LAND

PIET RETIEF

STANDERTON
MAR. 26TH

VRYHEID
MAR. 24TH

ESHOWE
MAR. 19TH

DURBAN
MAR. 20-23RD

LADYSMITH
MAR. 13TH

HARRISMITH
MAR. 13TH

BETHLEHEM
MAR. 10TH

ESTCOURT

GINGINDHLOVU

PIETERMARITZBURG
MAR. 18TH

N A T A L

S O U T H   A F R I C A

Natal
MAR. 14-17TH

Natal
Nat. Park
MAR. 11-12

MASERU MAR. 11TH

LADYBRAND
MAR. 11TH

B A S U T O L A N D

R. Caledon

Orange R.

UMTATA
MAR. 5TH

BUTTERWORTH

AMABELE

EAST LONDON
MAR. 1-4TH

KINGWILLIAMSTOWN
MAR. 4TH

QUEENSTOWN
MAR. 6TH

STERKSTROOM

LOVEDALE

ALICE
MAR. 1ST

GRAHAMSTOWN
FEB. 28TH

ALICEDALE
FEB. 28

PORT ELIZABETH
FEB. 26-28TH

KROONSTAD
MAR. 10TH

O R A N G E   F R E E   S T A T E

MAR. 8TH

Game
Reserve

BLOEMFONTEIN
MAR. 7-9TH

ALIWAL NORTH
MAR. 6TH

D r a

GRAAFF
REINET
FEB. 25TH

KLIPPLAAT

UITENHAGE

VRYBURG

Vaal R.

S O U T H   A F R I C A

O F

U N I O N

KIMBERLEY
APR. 18TH

DE AAR

G o o d

C A P E   O F   G O O D   H O P E

BEAUFORT WEST
APR. 19TH

G r e a t   K a r r o o

OUDTSHOORN
FEB. 24TH

WILDERNESS

GEORGE FEB. 24TH

MOSSEL BAY

STER
FEB. 22ND

SWELLENDAM

Orange R.

AFRICA

CAPE

D1357436

A
Re
Embarked Apr 24TH

M. Thompson.
Dec 6th 1944.

THE
ROYAL FAMILY
IN
AFRICA

By gracious permission of His Majesty the King, the Council of King George's Jubilee Trust have been authorized to prepare this record of the VISIT OF THE ROYAL FAMILY TO AFRICA

The Council express their cordial thanks to Mr. Walter Hutchinson, M.A., F.R.G.S., F.R.A.I., F.R.S.A., F.R.E.S., F.Z.S., Barrister-at-Law, Chairman and Managing Director of Hutchinson & Co. (Publishers) Ltd., who has produced this book, and who is devoting the proceeds to the funds of the Trust

The Royal party on arrival at Salisbury in Vikings of the King's Flight

THE
ROYAL FAMILY
IN
AFRICA

by

DERMOT MORRAH
(Late Fellow of All Souls College, Oxford)

With a Foreword by
FIELD-MARSHAL THE RT. HON.
J. C. SMUTS, O.M., C.H., F.R.S.
Prime Minister of the Union of South Africa

1947
HUTCHINSON & CO. (Publishers) LTD.
London   New York   Melbourne   Sydney   Cape Town

FOREWORD

By FIELD-MARSHAL
THE RT. HON. J. C. SMUTS, O.M., C.H., F.R.S.

WHEN in March 1946 the announcement was made that His Majesty The King had accepted our invitation to visit the Union in 1947, accompanied by Her Majesty The Queen and the two Princesses, it was received by our South African people with an enthusiasm that exceeded even my most optimistic expectations. And from the moment the Royal Family set foot on our shores it became clear that their journey through the Union was to be more of a sustained triumphal progress than the sort of visit we had originally planned.

The clamour to see the Royal Family was loud and insistent—and it came from every part of the population. Time after time—on some occasions quite late in the tour—the official programme was changed, at the King's request, to enable him to meet and greet sections of our people who felt that they might be overlooked. The King himself referred to the sincerity and catholicity of his welcome when he said in his farewell speech :

'Our journey through your land has been more than merely interesting and enjoyable, it has been made outstanding in our memories by the generous measure of loyalty and affection we have had the good fortune to receive from all sections of your people.'

It was indeed a remarkable event in our history and one of such importance that its effects can hardly yet be measured, and may be fully appreciated only with larger developments in the Commonwealth. We know that the friendliness of the King, the Queen's charm, and the winning simplicity of the two Princesses all made a deep and lasting impression upon our people. But we do feel that our lives, as ordinary citizens of the British Commonwealth, have been enriched by this human contact on a high level ; and that the grace and kindliness of the Royal Family have been a healing and reconciling influence on the differences which to some extent still unhappily distract us in this country.

It is fitting that an event such as this should receive permanent record. When the tour was being planned, we in South Africa considered whether we should produce our own official account of it. It was thought that a fair and objective account should be left to some experienced journalist who accompanied the Royal party—here is such an account by Mr. Dermot Morrah. Mr. Morrah had unique opportunities, not only of observing the events of the tour and the Royal Family both on and off duty, but also in seeing much of the country and establishing close contact with its people. His book is a fair and delightful account of what is indeed a great Commonwealth event, and will be welcomed by an even wider public who were interested in the Royal Tour of Southern Africa.

Investiture of Field-Marshal Smuts, O.M.

English Channel, February 1, 1947

THE ROYAL FAMILY IN AFRICA

MAJESTY AND DOMINION

"MAN," said the Greek philosopher Protagoras, "is the measure of all things." Exactly what Protagoras meant by these famous but cryptic words has been a matter of learned dispute ever since; the beauty of which is that the unlearned writer feels entitled to take them in any sense he pleases. Let us then apply them to politics, using that word also in the Greek sense, in which it means something larger than the mere science of government, being indeed the whole art of life by which men and women are enabled to dwell together in organized communities. In a political sense, then, the maxim of Protagoras may be taken to mean that the ultimate foundations of human society depend upon the right relation of personalities and not upon doctrines, documents, or abstract principles.

This is the idea that underlies monarchy— monarchy in all times and places, monarchy at all levels of civilization, but particularly monarchy in the British Empire to-day. We have no formal constitution; we rest our political life upon no abstract declaration of the social contract or the rights of man. Instead, every element in the most diverse and complex combination of races that has ever lived together within a single political system takes its place in the last resort by virtue of its relation to the King.

He is the man who is the measure of all British things. It is his function to humanize the corporate life of the whole Imperial Commonwealth. He represents the ultimate loyalties by which a society nourishes its highest aspirations—loyalties that are as simple as they are profound, but that tend to be cheapened or chilled when the lawyer or the philosopher attempts to reduce them to precise language on a graven tablet or a printed page.

So at least many English people think and most English people feel. We are well aware that beyond our imperial boundaries monarchy is out of fashion to-day. We observe that great modern communities, some of which have become more powerful than our own, have achieved stability by directing the allegiance of their peoples not to a person but to a document or an idea. "Whoso has never once felt the thrill of the word 'Republic'," says Mr. Geoffrey Dennis, "has not loved liberty enough." English people, who love liberty at least as well as any nation since the fall of Athens, are not likely to fail in their understanding of the proud idealism of the great republicans. Nevertheless it is very doubtful whether a system of government which has proved successful in the great continental territories of the United States and the Soviet Union, as it did in the little Greek cities long ago, could be successfully applied to a group of nations and races, professing a hundred religions, speaking four or five hundred languages, and scattered round the shores of all the oceans of the world.

In another book of this series some attention has been paid to the virtues of monarchy, in the writer's view the transcendent virtues, as a principle of society in a small island that history has made and kept united for a thousand years. Most of these virtues are of equal value in a scattered was developing, in the accidental British way, from a trading corporation into a government ruling enormous territories, very few Indians could attach any meaning to the idea that they owed allegiance to a board of directors or a body of shareholders, sitting in a distant island that they had never seen. It was only when they could personify their ultimate ruler under the individual name of "John Company" that they were able to find a focus for their loyalty. It is not generally known to English

Miniature Rifle Practice

empire; but in imperial government monarchy has still further advantages. It has a supreme simplicity, which enables men at every level of culture to share the same allegiance. It would be an interesting exercise in political casuistry to attempt to translate the Declaration of Independence or the manifesto of Karl Marx into terms that would win the devotion of a Maori or an Eskimo. The British Empire, in which these two peoples live, fortunately does not have to try. On a lower scale than that of sovereignty it has occasionally been faced with the insuperable difficulty of making abstractions plain to the comprehension of unsophisticated races. In the days when the East India Company people that this mysterious but very potent dignitary, John Company, had a first cousin in a country with which this book is to be principally concerned. The Dutch East India Company had precisely the same difficulty in making its nature understood by its primitive subjects in the East Indies and at the Cape of Good Hope. There also it was necessary to claim allegiance for an imaginary commanding personality, who naturally bore the name of "Jan Compagnie."

In the government of empires, then, the simplicity that the idea of monarchy can impart to politics is of supreme value. So the Romans felt, when the masterful hands of the Cæsars at last

At Sea

On Board H.M.S. Vanguard

grasped the reins that the galloping pace of imperial development had torn from the failing grasp of the aged Republic. So the British have found by experience. An indaba of half-naked Swazi warriors can with complete sincerity pay their homage to the ruler whom they conceive as the chief above all chiefs; and with equal sincerity a meeting of the Royal Society six thousand miles away can adopt a loyal address. It is doubtful whether the two assemblies could find a single other idea in common. Nor, of course, does the King himself mean the same thing to both of them. But for both the loyalty is the same. Each, vaguely or precisely according to the habit of his mind, can represent to himself the ultimate ideals binding together the community to which he feels he belongs; and each can declare his acceptance of those ideals by paying his homage to the same man.

This is the supreme service that monarchy renders to Empire, over and above the service that it renders to each separate nation or province of which Empire is made up. Ancient as the institution is, it has never looked less likely to become out of date. As the various peoples of the British

Commonwealth and Empire have advanced in the present century along the path to complete responsible self-government, which some of them have already attained, one after another the bonds uniting them to the government at Westminster have been by mutual consent untied. As each link that formerly represented the power of political control is dispensed with, the monarchy, which stands not for political control but for the acceptance of a common way of life, becomes steadily more important. In the case of the great self-governing Dominions it is all-important, for without it they would no longer be able to feel themselves parts of a single Commonwealth.

Ever since the British North America Act of 1867, which established the present constitution of Canada, it has been accepted by all progressive-minded students of politics that the leading British communities overseas must steadily advance in the practice and powers of self-government until they stand as fully equal partners with the people of the mother country.

Foreign critics declare over and over again that the completion of this process must mark the end of the unity of the Empire. The process was very near completion in 1914; but never was the unity of the Empire more apparent and more impregnable, to the confounding of its enemies, who had looked for its overthrow, than in the world struggle that began that year. At the end of the war the independence which in substance already existed, and in which it had been shown that confidence could be so implicitly placed, rapidly received formal recognition. The five Dominions, Canada, Newfoundland, Australia, New Zealand and South Africa, were accepted as sovereign members of the comity of nations by becoming foundation members of the League. As is usual in British affairs the theory waited for some time upon the fact; but the Imperial Conference of 1926 recommended legislation to make it quite clear that the partners in the Commonwealth were now "in every aspect of status equal and independent"; and this resolution was finally given the force of law by the Act known as the Statute of Westminster, 1931. The Statute finally ended what already had become in practice obsolete, the right of the Parliament at Westminster to pass acts binding the self-governing Dominions, save only by their own request and consent.

If the power of the Parliament of any one of the nations of the Commonwealth to interfere in the affairs of another has thus been terminated, it follows that every political connexion of less than parliamentary authority has also been brought to an end. But there is one institution in the Empire which is not indeed of higher authority than Parliament (for it is a part of Parliament), but which exercises its influence at a level above that of administration and law. The Statute of Westminster itself emphasizes the unique position of the monarchy by declaring in its preamble that henceforward no change ought to be made in the law touching the Crown, its title and rules of succession, without the separate consent of each of the sovereign partners whose equality the body

The Cruiser H.M.S. *Nigeria* arrives for escort duty off Freetown

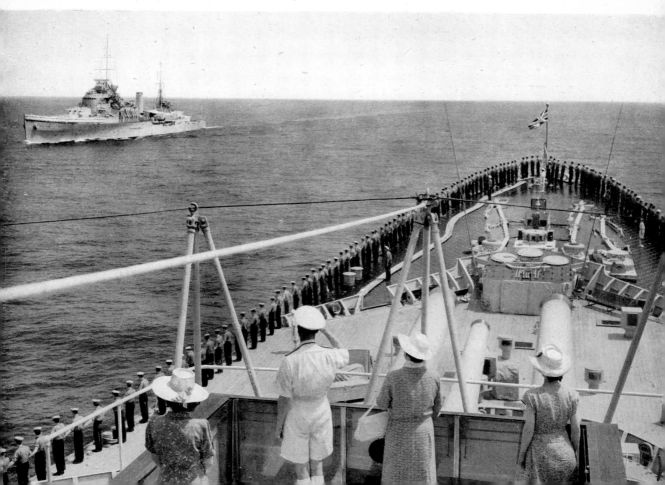

of the Act ratifies. Thus it is indirectly asserted that it is the monarchy and the monarchy alone that now embodies in institutional form the unity of the Empire. Once again hostile critics abroad declared with ostentatious confidence, on which they were foolish enough to base their foreign policy, that this imperial unity meant now no more than a scrap of paper and would collapse at the first strain. Once again it stood fast in the shock of battle and saved the liberties of the world. The second world war should have proved to

Rear-Admiral William G. Agnew
C.V.O., C.B., D.S.O.
Commanding H.M.S. *Vanguard*

the last of the sceptics that more powerful in the ultimate emergency than the rule of force, or even the rule of law, is the shared devotion to a single ideal of liberty, toleration, and justice—everything that for the peoples of the imperial allegiance is summed up and represented in the person of the King.

But it is vital to the work of monarchy to appreciate that this devotion, which can hold fast in the hurricanes of war where all merely legal bonds would snap, is paid by the vast

majority of men and women, not to the abstraction that we call the Crown, but to the human personality of the King himself. It may fade and ultimately fail if the King is allowed to become so remote from any of the peoples who are ruled in his name that they come at last to think of him as a mere symbol, like the throne he occupies or the crown he wears. It is the consciousness of personality that gives kingship its dominion in the hearts of men; and that consciousness, though it may be kept alive for years by loyal imagination, needs the stimulus of sight. Those of the King's subjects who have the good fortune to live in England, where he is amongst them and will at least be seen occasionally by most of them, may not always realize what a strain is placed upon the loyalty of their fellow subjects across the oceans, who for a personal focus of their patriotism have to depend upon pictures and an occasional paragraph in the newspapers about the doings of royalty.

It was just that the people of the United Kingdom during the war should enjoy the unique

The Royal Party

encouragement of the presence of their King and Queen among them, for theirs was the greatest danger and the greatest need. But they, who know best the warmth and colour that the gracious influence of a royal family like ours infuses into a nation's life, should be the first to realize how necessary these things are for the enrichment of living among peoples far away, who have now an equal claim with themselves, even in law, upon the royal favour. The King in the modern Empire is not the repository of supreme power; he is the embodiment of the nation's ideals, existing to make them visible. And therefore he must be seen

bosom of a single State." In South Africa, however, there have been at least four nations, perhaps even five. It is not surprising that the achievement of national unity, which even in Canada is incomplete, still lags far behind in this, the youngest of the self-governing Dominions.

The slowness of the process of fusing the races of South Africa into a single community arises largely from the fact that the first European discoverers of the country treated it only as a means to an end. Bartholomew Diaz rounded the Cape of Good Hope in 1486; Vasco da Gama made the passage to India in 1497; Saldanha made the first

South African Escort in Table Bay

to be believed. King George VI before the second world war had been seen, though not yet as King, by the people of Australia and New Zealand; he had been seen as King in Canada; but he had never been seen in South Africa. Yet in some ways South Africa's was the greatest need.

Of all the ideas for which the King stands, the most vital perhaps in modern conditions is that of unity; and South Africa has had more difficulty in achieving unity, either among the sections of its own population, or between itself and the rest of the Commonwealth, than any other Dominion. The reasons are rooted deep in history. In 1839 Lord Durham defined what was then considered the intractable problem of Canadian unity by saying "I found two nations warring in the

landing in Table Bay in 1503. All these great Portuguese mariners were looking for the fabulous riches of the Indies, and the Cape was to them only a step on the way. When King John of Portugal bestowed upon it its present name, in place of the grim "Cape of Storms" of Diaz, he was thinking of the hope of Indian gold rather than a place of settlement for his own people. In fact, the Portuguese never attempted to settle at the Cape. That was left for the Dutch in the seventeenth century; and even they only settled as a matter of second thoughts. The Dutch East India Company, trading mainly to the East Indies, required a revictualling station for their ships half-way on the long voyage, and in 1652 they sent out a party, headed by a ship's surgeon named Jan van Riebeek, to establish it. Gradually the little community of the company's servants, living at the foot of Table Mountain where Cape Town now stands, found it economically impossible to sustain themselves unless they increased their numbers and entered upon the cultivation of the land. So the revictualling station inevitably developed into a colony. One of the four races of the modern Union of South Africa had arrived.

They did not, as is commonly supposed, find what are now called the native races already in possession. The inhabitants of the Cape Province in the seventeenth century were a sparse population of Bushmen and Hottentots, both races already on the decline. Neither of them survives in appreciable numbers to-day. Cape Town, being the central where its few survivors now exist as nomad hunters, scarcely approachable by civilized men. Thus there grew up around and about Table Mountain the peculiar mixed race known as "the Cape Coloured," which, though it can scarcely be ranked as one of the nations of Africa, yet retains a character of its own which sharply differentiates it from either the white or the entirely black. Its language is the derivative of Dutch which is called Afrikaans; and its religion is Christian, except for a small section which has remained faithful to Islam and constitutes a distinct community within the Cape Coloured race under the name of Malays.

During the seventeenth century, while the Dutch were gradually and rather reluctantly striking their roots into African soil, dark-skinned races from

The Arrival.

port of call of the whole of the southern hemisphere, rapidly developed that characteristic feature of a great harbour, an extremely mixed population. It was long known as "the tavern of the seas." To it drifted all manner of people, great numbers of Javanese and Malayans from the commercial Empire that the Dutch East India Company was building up in the Pacific and Indian Oceans, and many varieties of negroes who were brought down from the East and West coasts of Africa as slaves. In the early days of the settlement very few women came out from the Netherlands; and the inevitable result was that the blood of the white race was to some extent intermingled with that of the black. All the black races intermarried with one another and with the indigenous Hottentots—to some extent with the Bushmen, although that extremely primitive race was for the most part driven out into the wildest and remotest parts of South-West Africa, probably north of the equator were pressing steadily southward in one of those great migrations which so largely determine the course of history. These races are now collectively known as Bantu, and include the Zulu, the Mashona, the Matabele, the Swazi, the Bechuana, the Basuto, the Xosa, the Fingo, and, in fact, nearly all the native races which there will be occasion to mention in this book. The significant fact to remember is that during the seventeenth and eighteenth centuries the Bantu from the North and the Europeans from the South were both pressing into an almost empty land. The clash between them was not to come till considerably later. Now that they have met and mingled, with severe friction of which the end is not yet, it is only just to observe that neither of them has any better right than the other to claim the title of original possessor of the country. In its northern

The King and His Lieutenant: Mr. Brand Van Zyl, Governor-General of the Union, welcomes His Majesty to South Africa

regions the Bantu entered first, in its southern the Afrikaner; but, taking the country as a whole, the two races came in as invaders at about the same time. The second of the four nations of South Africa is the Bantu.

Although Sir Francis Drake rounded the Cape in 1580 and James Lancaster landed in Table Bay in 1591, the English connexion with South Africa is a thing of comparatively recent growth. It is became more intense. It was essential that Table Bay, if not in British, should at least be in friendly hands. In 1794 the Dutch East India Company became finally bankrupt. Pitt's Government, apprehensive lest the great harbour should fall into the hands of revolutionary France, which had been at war with England since 1793, ordered a squadron to occupy Cape Town, as the allies and protectors of the Dutch, in 1795. It is not

His Majesty and the Prime Minister

true that two officers of the English East India Company took it upon themselves in 1620 to annex the Cape Peninsula; but King James I, at his wits' end to extract money from his Parliament and therefore most reluctant to challenge the other maritime nations to a conflict for supremacy in the South Atlantic, did not ratify the annexation. But after the Treaty of Utrecht in 1713, as the sea power of the Netherlands began to decline through the sheer exhaustion of even a victorious war, and the British Navy and Merchant Marine more and more tended to fill the void that was left, British interest in the key points of the ocean highways necessary here to enter into the complex military history of the port during the twenty-two years of the revolutionary and Napoleonic wars. The Netherlands changed from side to side in the course of the conflict; the British first evacuated and then reoccupied Cape Town. But in the eventual settlement by the Treaty of Vienna in 1814, which was left undisturbed by the second Treaty of Paris after Waterloo, Cape Town and all the territories surrounding it which had been so far settled by Europeans remained under the British flag. So the third of the great races of the land came to South Africa.

The coming of the English, with vastly greater resources behind them than had belonged to the Dutch East India Company in its decline, was the beginning of a rapid extension of the white man's hold upon Southern Africa. The now heavy pressure of the Bantu races on the eastern frontier of Cape Colony soon made it clear to the Government at home that the white population must be reinforced if it were not to perish; and in 1820 a considerable body of young and vigorous people was sent out at government expense to land where now stands the great harbour of Port Elizabeth, and to settle upon and till such land as by their own efforts they were able to defend. These adventurous pioneers, still known as the 1820 settlers, hold a romantic place in the traditions of South Africa. But their coming made a marked change in the relations between the two white races. The English were no longer a governing caste in a Dutch land; they had become farmers side by side with the older inhabitants, and were rapidly attaining a numerical equality with them.

In the next generation, therefore, the relation between the English and the Dutch became increasingly uneasy. Both were ancient and proud peoples with their own long-established habits of life, and they could not settle down easily together. The Dutch especially were haunted by the fear that their own treasured tradition and culture, based upon the Calvinist religion and the peasant habits of the European Netherlands, would be overwhelmed by the sheer weight of resources commanded by the British colonies. Moreover, the pattern of their life had been formed in Africa during centuries in which the national economy had been founded unashamedly upon the institution of slavery. When in 1833 slavery was abolished throughout the British Empire, the money compensation given to the slave owners failed to satisfy the Afrikaner farmers; and the revolution that seemed to be portended in the relation between the European and native races was deeply resented by many. The increased cost of agricultural production added itself to various pre-existing grievances; and the remedy, for a people whose custom, differing from the English law of primogeniture, had always been to divide up their estates among their numerous children, seemed to be to seek more land, preferably where the alien legal system did

Cape Town: the processional entry

not apply. Loading themselves, their wives and children, and all their portable possessions upon the great ox-drawn wagons which were then the sole means of transport across the trackless wilds of Africa, parties, sometimes of two or three families, sometimes of hundreds, set off to seek their fortune in the unknown interior.

This movement, which was at its greatest intensity between 1835 and 1840, but which is in the blood of the Boers and even now has scarcely come to an end, is known in history as the Great Trek. The trekkers endured unimaginable hardships as they dragged their unwieldy wagons over the perilous passes of the Drakensberg mountains; many of them were slaughtered in battle or by treachery by the savage races among whom they had to move. But in the great victory of Blood River on December 16, 1838, the main body of trekkers, led by Andries Pretorius, totally defeated the *impis* of the Zulu King Dingaan and established such respect for their military prowess that from then on their settlement in the lands beyond the Orange and Vaal Rivers was comparatively unmolested. In time they established themselves in two new states, the Orange Free State and the Transvaal, which they declared to be independent republics and where they hoped to be able to carry on the old Afrikaner life undisturbed by the intrusive English to the south.

The complicated history of South Africa in the nineteenth century turns largely upon the continuous struggle of the two Boer republics to maintain their isolation, and upon the spasmodic efforts of the British authorities in Whitehall and Cape Town to bring back under control communities to whose fortunes they could not be indifferent, owing to the constant tension between the Boers and the native races on their frontiers. The English had a good case in law, since legally the trekkers, who were originally British subjects, were not entitled to forswear their allegiance unless they chose to become subjects of the native potentates into whose lands they had migrated. The Boers may well be thought to have had a better moral case, for the lands on which they now dwelt they had won for themselves without British help, and they asked only to live their own lives in their own way at peace. But there was no peace. Three races and not two were involved; and in order to sustain themselves against the Bantu the republics were

bound to lean upon British power and so give a handle to British intervention. Policy vacillated. At one time the British Government annexed the republics; at another it restored their independence but retained them under "protection." Meanwhile a second colony under direct British rule was growing up on the east coast after the annexation of Natal in 1844. This colony, like the Cape, was of mixed blood; its capital, Pietermaritzburg, was actually founded by the trekkers, and in its name commemorates one of their most famous leaders. But the colony has always been economically dominated by the great port of Durban, which has been developed almost entirely by British enterprise; and to-day the predominance of British blood and influence is more marked in Natal than anywhere else in South Africa.

The tension between the two white cultures was suddenly increased and complicated by the discovery of gold on the Witwatersrand in 1884. That event, which in a few years converted a ramshackle miners' camp into the extensive and populous city of Johannesburg, brought about the influx of a great new population, mostly British subjects, and made the isolation of the Trekker republics henceforth untenable. The Boer authorities of the Transvaal, not unnaturally resenting the sudden intrusion into their midst of many thousands of alien speculators, denied the newcomers, known as Uitlanders, all political rights; the Uitlanders, very conscious that their new industry was henceforth the financial foundation of the country's prosperity, relied on the British Government at Cape Town to secure for them political authority commensurate with their economic importance. The great Prime Minister of the Cape Colony, Cecil Rhodes, wholeheartedly supported them; with equal resolution the venerable President of the Transvaal, Paul Kruger, who in his childhood had himself been a trekker, based upon the repression of the Uitlanders his whole defence of the old pastoral civilization of the Boers. So at last in 1899 the long-smouldering animosity between the two white races of South Africa blazed up into war.

It has been called the last of the gentlemen's wars. In its first stages the Boers, mainly by their superior veldcraft, fine marksmanship, and intimate understanding of the country in which they fought, subjected the greatly superior forces of the

Cape Town
by night

Cape Town: the state banquet

British to a series of humiliating defeats. In the end, wealth and numbers inevitably told, and the gallant Afrikaners were overborne. But, in the three years that elapsed before the Boer leaders made their submission at Vereeniging in May 1902, each side had learned a wholesome respect for the character as well as the military capacity of the other; and the mutual understanding that comes sometimes of the chivalrous relations between opposed soldiers in the field may well be thought to have set the feet of the two peoples more firmly upon the road to reconciliation than all the perplexed diplomacy of the nineteenth-century colonial Governors and republican Presidents.

The sequel to the war is one of the most remarkable episodes in the history of the British Empire, and the real beginning of the new liberal imperialism. The two republics were necessarily annexed; so much was the inevitable consequence of their defeat. For a few years crown-colony government was established in the Transvaal and what was called the Orange River Colony. But within three years of the signing of peace a Boer deputation

was in London to plead for the restoration of self-government. A young lawyer whom the war had made into a general, named Jan Christiaan Smuts, went to see a young war correspondent whom the peace had made into a Minister, named Winston Spencer Churchill, and put the case for self-government to him. Mr. Churchill replied that there was no precedent in history for such treatment of a defeated enemy; General Smuts retorted that this was not a matter of history but of the future of a nation, and appealed to the Prime Minister, Sir Henry Campbell-Bannerman. In the end the Cabinet accepted his plea, and, since Mr. Churchill remained a member of it, he must be presumed, not for the only time in his career, to have changed his mind. In 1906 responsible self-government under the Crown was conceded to the Transvaal and to the Orange River Colony, which soon reverted to its old name.

In 1910, persuaded by the far-seeing statesmanship of Lord Selborne, who declared that if the four colonies remained separate they

Westbrook: the Governor General's garden party

would inevitably be fighting one another again in a few years, Cape Colony, Natal, the Transvaal, and the Orange Free State entered into an agreement to unite in a single state. That state, which was and is called the Union of South Africa, was constituted by Act of the Imperial Parliament, and endowed with all the institutions of Cabinet and parliamentary self-government which had grown up in the course of centuries in the British Isles. Under the central government each of the four colonies, now called provinces, retained its own executive and legislature for the management of its local affairs. In the whole Union there was an Afrikaner majority in the electorate. Thus it came about that, within less than nine years from the

misunderstanding between them persisted. War, even "a gentlemen's war," leaves its inevitable bitterness behind.

The actual fighting men might have made up their quarrel; but the children who had been orphaned by the struggle, not only those whose fathers had been killed in the field, but those whose mothers had died in the epidemics at the concentration camps, where the British generals with the best intentions had placed the Boer women for safety while their husbands were on commando—this second generation as it grew up inherited animosities that were difficult to allay. At the outbreak of war in 1914 a section of the Boer people, not yet reconciled to defeat, rose

Cape Town: in the grounds of Government House

British victory over the Boers, the whole people of South Africa, British and Dutch, were being ruled by a Government depending mainly upon the votes of the vanquished, and headed by Louis Botha, the most illustrious of the defeated generals. The records of war may be searched in vain for such an act of generosity and trust on the part of the conquerors; and the response on the part of the Afrikaner people has shown that the generosity is appreciated and the trust is rightly placed. In two world wars the loyalty of the Union of South Africa to the British Crown has been a bulwark for the liberties of the world.

But although English and Afrikaans-speaking South Africans had agreed to live together as members of a single state, they remained two races and not one; and the old sources of

in revolt. Louis Botha, punctiliously using only Afrikaner troops, lest any excuse should be given for reviving the old feud between the races, restored the authority of the Union Government and the British Crown. In 1939 the internal peace of the country was never threatened. But between the wars its politics were mainly governed by the old question whether the Afrikaner culture could be contained within the system of the British Empire, or would assert the right of its superior numbers to break away and pursue its future in isolation.

There is a strong trend among the Afrikaans-speaking people which takes the view that the maintenance of its essential character demands the utmost dissociation from the British connexion; and many of these are dissatisfied even with the

Cape Town: the floodlights

which had fought on the English side in the war, the Cape Colony and Natal, with the two former republics, the Transvaal and the Orange Free State. It was of the first importance that neither group should feel that it had been made subordinate to the other. If the capital had been fixed in one of them, the other would have had a justifiable grievance. Accordingly there are two capitals; in a sense there are even three. The Parliament of the Union sits at Cape Town, but the executive government is carried on from Pretoria, the capital of the Transvaal and the seat of Kruger's government during the war. Bloemfontein, where the supreme court sits, may be considered a third or judicial capital. English and Afrikaans have equal status as official languages, both are taught in the schools, and holders of appointments under government are required to be proficient in both. There are two national anthems, "God Save the King" and "Die Stem van Suid Afrika," a hymn definitely designed to be acceptable to republican sentiment, in which the

sovereign independence under the Crown which comes with dominion status, and claim to set up a separate Republic of South Africa. The Nationalist Party, which is the official opposition and the alternative government to-day, is not formally committed to the full policy of separation, but includes large numbers of republicans in its ranks. Republicanism in the extreme sense is probably now a declining force. But even if it is rejected, a fundamental choice confronts South Africa concerning the ultimate relation between the speakers of English and of Afrikaans. Are two separate cultures and ways of life to survive side by side in mutual respect, or are the two to become ultimately fused in a single South African nationalism? For the sake of the greatness of South Africa in the world it would seem that the second is the preferable solution; but Afrikaner patriots who still love the ancient ways, and are still obsessed with the natural defensiveness of a small people confronting the might of a great Empire, may be forgiven if they use all their efforts to retard the process of absorption.

The division between the white races, which was still acute at the date of Union, has left its mark deeply imprinted upon the constitution of the country. The Union combined two provinces

Cape Town: before the state banquet

Coloured ball, Cape Town: the Malays

name of the King is not mentioned. There are even two flags, the Union Jack, which is common to the whole Empire, and a flag the design of which emerged from a heated controversy when the Nationalist party was in power in 1928. Its principal colours are the blue, white and orange of the old republics; but to meet the resolute contention of the opposition of those days, especially in Natal, that the Union Jack must form at least a part of the design, the white stripe is charged with three smaller flags, the Union Jack, and those of the Transvaal and the Free State.

Thus at every turn in the Union of South Africa one is reminded officially that this is a land in which two distinct white races maintain their separate ideals and have still to find the final terms on which they may share the country. There are far fewer signs that there are also other and more numerous races in the land. Except in Cape Colony, which inherits the traditions of liberal colonial administration of the mid-nineteenth century, the franchise is confined to the white races. Everywhere the natives are excluded from nearly all forms of skilled employment; and partly for their own protection, lest they be driven off the land by the competition of the more favoured white, a very large proportion of them live in so-called native reserves, where land holding is confined to their own race. From the reserves they may come in as labourers to work in the white man's industries, especially the mines; but they leave their families to maintain the cultivation of the land and return to them after a season's employment. The fundamental fact about the social order of the Union, a fact that sharply distinguishes it from that of most of the British colonies in Africa, is that the white and black races are permanently in competition for the soil, and no final equilibrium has been established between them. Meanwhile the white man rules; but his numbers are less than three million in a total population of eleven million. With the native races of all Africa steadily advancing in education and in acquaintance with European political thought, the future relations of the races in the Union are beyond any man's power to foretell.

Complicated as this situation is, it has been given further complexity in the last three generations by the addition of an Asiatic element to the European and African races already contending for the land. In the 1860's the sugar-planters of Natal, finding it difficult to obtain all the native labour they required, began to introduce Indians under indenture to help till their fields. Many of these Indians settled in the country after their indentures had expired; they increased and multiplied exceedingly; being the intellectual superiors of the natives, and having a lower standard of living than the Europeans, they have acquired almost a monopoly of many forms of retail trade. Down to about 1923 their numbers in Natal actually exceeded those of the Europeans. Alarmed at the prospect of being swamped, the purely European legislature of Natal has passed a series of restrictive enactments to prevent the acquisition of land by Indians; and the long dispute thence arising has eventually involved the Government of the Union in a quarrel with India itself. This quarrel was in an acute phase at the time when the King arrived in South Africa, and the Natal Indian Congress asserted its grievance by calling upon its constituents to boycott the royal tour.

Thus it was to a land sorely riven by divisions which had come down to it from a stormy past, and for which no living person or group could be held mainly responsible, that the Royal Family were invited by its Prime Minister and Cabinet. There was no country in the Empire that stood so much in need of the reconciling and healing influence that it is the special function of modern royalty to impart. At the same time it was the only one of his self-governing Dominions with which His Majesty was unacquainted; and no doubt the invitation extended by General Smuts at the end of the war was particularly welcome on that account. It could have been, but probably was not, couched in the form of technical constitutional "advice," which the King is by convention bound to take; for under the Statute of Westminster the King's Ministers in a Dominion have now an equal right with those of the United Kingdom to advise him. Although in so personal a matter General Smuts would scarcely have stood upon this punctilio, the immediate acceptance of the invitation was a graceful acknowledgment of the fact that the King no longer belongs in any special sense to the United Kingdom, but that all the Dominions have an equal claim upon him. The full and frank acceptance of this doctrine

Morning tea-party above Paarl

was emphasized by the King's decision that the whole Royal Family, for the first time in the history of the Empire, should make the journey together, and that it should be so timed that a family event of the highest importance, the coming-of-age of the Heiress Presumptive, should be celebrated on South African soil. It was the King and Queen of South Africa, an intimate part of the body politic of the Union, and not the sovereign and consort of some remote and alien governing power, who came to greet and be greeted by the members of the great and heterogeneous African family of which by birth they were the heads.

CAPE PROVINCE

CAPE TOWN is the mother city of South Africa. Its cardinal position in the southern world is marked by the hand of nature with the mighty monument of Table Mountain, which Drake in 1580, when he sighted it in the course of his circumnavigation of the globe, described as "a most statelie thing, and the fairest Cape we saw in the whole circumference of the earth." Where the lovely curve of the bay at its foot invited the first explorers to one of the finest anchorages in the southern hemisphere, the mountain itself, as the mariner sees it from his deck at dawn, seems a vast and impregnable rampart, barring the way into the dark mysteries

Cape Town: leaving the Houses of Parliament

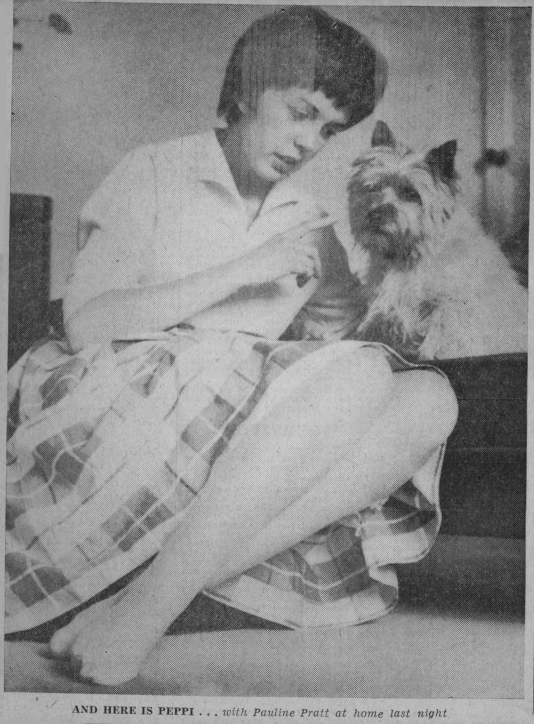

AND HERE IS PEPPI . . . *with Pauline Pratt at home last night*

found

...erted ship

...not now carry a single soul aboard. . . .

The Dei Gratia took the Mary Celeste in tow, and a few days later brought her into Gibraltar Harbour.

Then began the great inquiry. The Mary Celeste had been under the command of 37-year-old Captain Benjamin Briggs, who was highly regarded both for his nautical skill and his moral character. He had bought a share in her.

NO DRINKING

He had with him his wife and their two-year-old daughter, and a crew of seven. These have sometimes been described as hooligans and brigands. There is nothing in their records to justify this.

And although her cargo was 1,700 barrels of alcohol, Captain Briggs imposed a strict no-drinking rule.

The Mary Celeste (NOT Marie Celeste, as popular usage has it)

left New York on November 5, 1872, for Genoa.

For two days, because of bad weather, Captain Briggs decided to stand off Staten Island.

Then, on November 7, the Mary Celeste weighed anchor and headed in fine weather across the Atlantic.

THE LOG

The next eighteen days can easily be pictured through the laconic record of the log. "E.S.E."; "9 knots"; "Rainy"; "Comes in fresh"; "Got in Royals and top G. sail"—in these routine memoranda are reflected the customary life of a sailing crew at work; checking the course, assessing the rate of progress, watching the weather, performing the hundred and one recurrent jobs of navigation.

The omissions in the log are as significant as the entries. Mutely they betoken a passage—so far—entirely commonplace and unremarkable.

Then the log ended.

Ten days later, she was 380 miles from the last position given in her log, and doubling on her tracks.

What happened? What *might* have happened? What *could* have happened?

SURVIVORS

There have been claims by a number of people that they were survivors of the Mary Celeste.

They have produced colourful accounts of escapes from various emergencies. The only trouble is that no two accounts of what happened are in agreement.

No serious investigator gives any credence to these claims.

Dozens of explanations have been put f o r w a r d, some obviously crackpot: the ship was attacked by a sea-serpent; a cloud of poison gas from an undersea explosion panicked all aboard into jumping into the sea. . . .

MUTINY?

Of the remaining theories, nearly all collapse in the face of known facts. Only three merit serious consideration.

THEORY ONE is mutiny. It is suggested that the crew disposed of the officers, the woman, and the child and then made

TOP
FASHION
IS THE
'UNSEEN SO

The King with his South African Cabinet

Front row, left to right: The Hon. J. W. Mushet, Minister of Posts and Telegraphs; The Hon. F. C. Sturrock, Minister of Transport; Field-Marshal The Rt. Hon. J. C. Smuts, O.M., Prime Minister, Minister of External Affairs and Defence; His Majesty the King; The Rt. Hon. J. H. Hofmeyr, Minister of Finance and Education; The Hon. H. G. Lawrence, Minister of Justice, Social Welfare and Demobilization; Senator The Hon. A. M. Conroy, Minister of Lands. *Back row, left to right:* Dr. The Hon C. F. Steyn, Minister of Labour; The Hon C. F. Waterson, Minister of Economic Development and Mines; Major The Hon. P. V. G. van der Byl, Minister of Native Affairs; The Hon. J. C. N. Strauss, Minister of Agriculture; Dr. The Hon. H. Gluckman, Minister of Health

of Africa. It is, however, no mere mass of barren rock. Its precipices are clothed with forests of many kinds of trees; a rich variety of gorgeous flowers light up their shadows; and as sun and moon shine upon the mountain's bulk, as the clouds cling about its flat summit and come cascading over the edge, or the wind ripples the leaves of the silver-trees, the ever-changing hues give to its outline a variety and charm that never grow stale. There are men and women in Cape Town who have fallen in love with Table Mountain and spend every free day of their lives exploring its secrets—secrets that no one ever entirely masters.

Between the mountain and the bay the city has spread its streets through the slow processes of three hundred years. Much of it is ill-planned and meanly constructed; that is inevitable in a town that has grown up haphazard to meet the needs of work-a-day life. But it also possesses noble buildings: the stern seventeenth-century Castle

which was built for the Dutch Governors; the simple white-gabled mansion which was originally the guest house of the Dutch East India Company and is now the official residence of the Governor-General; the still more perfect specimen near by of the old colonial style of architecture which is known as the Old Court House, though it has now been taken over by government departments; and outside the city to the east the University Buildings on their slope overlooking the sea, the Prime Minister's house of Groote Schuur, and Sir Herbert Baker's lordly memorial to Cecil Rhodes. In the city also are the Houses of Parliament, the buildings of the Provincial Government, two cathedrals, one of the Anglican and the other of the Roman obedience, and among modern secular buildings a fine and dignified pile which houses the General Post Office.

In modern times Cape Town has become the centre of a group of suburbs or satellite towns which have spread themselves round the beautiful bays on the three sides of the peninsula on which it stands. They front three oceans, the Atlantic, the Antarctic, and the Indian; and they are at the same time the homes of the working population of the capital and pleasure resorts for holiday makers from all over the Cape Province and beyond. At the time the King and Queen arrived the summer holiday season was not yet over, and these towns, Muizenberg, St. James, Fish Hoek, and others extending twenty miles from the city, were crowded with residents and visitors. On the

Family had accepted the Government's invitation in March 1946. An unending series of articles in the press, followed in more recent months by all the excitement of decorating the city, buying new clothes, and speculating on who would be fortunate enough to receive invitations to state functions, all these things had raised expectation to a feverish temperature. For most people born and bred in South Africa it all seemed a little unreal. Throughout their lives the King had been to them a half-mythical figure, a mysterious

Cape Town: departure of the White Train

night of February 16 they were pouring their inhabitants into Cape Town, to swell the multitudes of the city's own population, many of whom spent the whole night in the streets to make sure of a clear view. In the early morning, as soon as the suburban train services began to run, thousands more came flocking in, casting anxious glances at the sky, for the notorious south-easter of the Cape had been blowing over the weekend, and all Cape Town had been praying that the wind would drop in time to welcome the visitors with the royal splendour of its summer sunshine.

This was a moment for which South Africa had been waiting for nearly a year, since the Royal

abstraction in whose name they were governed, whose effigy appeared on their coins, but whom it was difficult to think of as a creature of flesh and blood. People were prepared for the pomp and circumstance of the royal visit, and had been assiduously practising their bows and curtsies; those who occupied high official positions had been rather anxiously rehearsing their speeches of welcome. Though South Africans are not naturally a ceremonious people, they felt that in dealing with these formalities they knew roughly what to expect. What they were inclined to take with a good deal of suspicion was the long-continued effort by so many writers in the newspapers, some of them claiming direct acquaintance with the

On the engine of the White Train

way at half-past eight, four distant figures emerged on a high platform above the great guns of the forward turret. It was South Africa's first glimpse of the Royal Family, and from the moment they became visible the Queen was seen to be waving greetings to her people. A great cheer went up from the shore, and some of those who were acquainted with both parties to this historic meeting felt it an auspicious omen that this first interchange of compliments should take so kindly and human a form, and that the solemnities of state reception should necessarily come later on. Already the conception of royalty as a graven image was beginning to dissolve.

South Africa, however, was determined not to fail in its ceremonial duties to its illustrious visitors. As H.M.S. *Vanguard* floated majestically on towards the quay, her company in tropical rig lining the decks, Cabinet Ministers and other dignitaries of the land were gathering on a circular

Royal Family in England, to persuade them that King, Queen and Princesses were a family of simple human beings, sharing the feelings and emotions of ordinary people like themselves. This seemed to many of them rather difficult to believe; but they were determined to show their loyalty to the institution, and as to the persons they would wait and see.

By the time the sun rose, the streets along which the royal procession would pass were packed with people, and every seat on the tall stands that enclosed a great oblong at the Duncan Dock was filled. To the delight of everybody the day broke calm and clear. Table Mountain stood in crystalline majesty against a blue sky, clean-cut as a painting by Canaletto; no cloud lay like a table-cloth on its surface or trickled in misty cataracts over the edge. In Table Bay the grey and silver bulk of the greatest of British battleships, H.M.S. *Vanguard*, the gaiety of her bunting contrasting with the grimness of her mighty guns, lay motionless on a shimmering sea. For the first time South Africans saw, flapping idly in a light breeze, the gold and gules and azure of the Royal Banner (or standard) which flies to denote the presence of the Sovereign in person. The raising and lowering of that historic flag, on the long circuit of ten thousand miles, would in the coming months be the outward and visible sign of the passage of the King of South Africa through the length and breadth of his Dominion. From the upper yard-arms flew the Admiralty flag and the Union Jack.

From the stands innumerable field glasses and telescopes were trained upon the ship, and, as she slowly got under

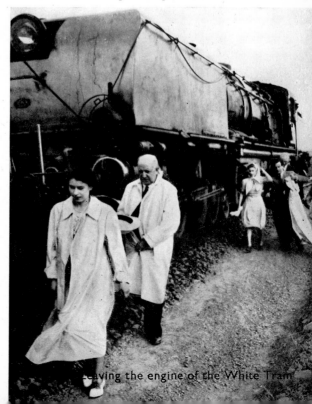

Leaving the engine of the White Train

dais, red-carpeted and white-canopied, close to the spot where she would be berthed. A guard of honour from the South African Navy, led by a Marine band, marched on to the parade ground. The cheering from the stands was echoed by other cheers from far back in the city, as General Smuts drove down to take his place at the head of his Cabinet colleagues on the dais, and was closely followed by Meneer Brand van Zyl, the Governor-General who exercises in the King's absence the powers of royalty in the Union, and Mrs. van Zyl.

The bands ashore struck up the two national anthems; first "God Save the King," and then "Die Stem van Suid Afrika." They were not playing for King George but for the Governor-General, still for a few minutes the visible head of the South African State. Then Meneer van Zyl and General Smuts went up the gangway, accompanied by the chief military commanders of the Union, to be the first to greet their Sovereign and in symbolic form submit their delegated authority to the power from which it was derived. They passed out of sight for a few moments, and then the King appeared on deck and proceeded to inspect the ship's guard of honour. As he passed along the ranks the two national anthems were played again by the Marine band on board; and perhaps it was now that he for the first time heard "Die Stem van Suid Afrika" played as a personal salute to himself. He would hear it many hundred times more in the coming months.

On the broad slopes of Signal Hill thousands of school children formed with their white-clad bodies the word "Welcome," and more solemnly the guns boomed out their salute as for the first time in history a reigning sovereign set his foot on South African soil. There was another guard of honour to inspect on shore; but Their Majesties instantly set the tone of the whole visit by cutting short the ceremonies of presentation and in a few moments drawing the whole of the distinguished company on the dais into easy and informal talk. Then, taking their places in an open car, while the Princesses followed in another, they began their processional drive into the legislative capital. A dozen more motor cars fell into column behind them, containing members of the royal household, South African Ministers, and lesser persons officially connected with the tour. Up the broad straight streets of the city they passed at a walking pace, seeing first the bronze statue of Jan van Riebeek, where he stands gazing northwards towards the Netherlands as if commemorating the old allegiance, making detours, first west, then east towards the Castle, back into Adderley Street, the principal commercial thoroughfare, and so at last, between the Houses of Parliament and the Cathedral, into the avenue of oaks planted by Governor Simon van der Stel nearly three hundred years ago. Wherever they passed the streets were lined with troops or boy scouts, behind whom dense throngs drawn from all the multifarious races of South Africa cheered and cheered again, while above, on the balconies that are so characteristic of South African towns, companies nearly as closely packed waved their flags and handkerchiefs and shouted their greetings until they were hoarse. So the King and Queen with their daughters were taken to the heart of the mother city, and withdrew for a little while to rest at Government House before beginning the great state functions belonging to their office.

For three and a half days the Royal Family remained in Cape Town, while a crowded programme of ceremonial and social events unfolded itself, the purpose of which was double: first, to enable the people of South Africa, through their constitutional representatives, to perform all those acts of solemn obeisance by which loyalty is expressed and the glory of a great dominion symbolized to the minds of men; and secondly, as near as possible to the level of familiar contact, to enable the Royal Family to see and be seen by the greatest possible number of their South African subjects of every race. This two-fold purpose would indeed pervade the entire programme of the tour of South Africa; it was necessary to exhibit everywhere both the august symbol of the Crown and the friendly personality of its wearer. When the people could feel in their hearts that the two were different aspects of the same creative idea, they would have learned the inward meaning of modern monarchy and its power to humanize politics and uplift a nation's social life.

The first ceremony was of a kind commonly performed on occasions of great rejoicing in England. It had, for instance, taken place twice in 1945, in celebration of victory, first over Germany and then over Japan. The two Houses of Parliament came in procession to Government House

Children's Floral Pageant at Grayville Racecourse

(which is next door to the Houses of Parliament) to present loyal addresses to the Sovereign who is himself an integral part of every Parliament in the Commonwealth. The King, with the Queen beside him, received them in the white and gold ballroom of Government House, and after thanking them for their welcome made a happy addition of his own to the official programme. He called the Prime Minister, General Smuts, up to the throne and slipped over his head the ribbon of the Order of Merit, which had been awarded to him in the New Year Honours List. The little ceremony was a pleasing token of the progress of reconciliation in fifty years of South African history, for it seemed finally to seal the relationship between the King and the man who was now his chief confidential adviser and friend in South Africa, although he had been one of the most brilliant of the commanders in arms against Queen Victoria in those old unhappy days.

In the afternoon the foreign diplomats accredited to the South African Government, gorgeous figures wearing the ribbons and stars of half the European orders of chivalry, came to pay their respects; and in the evening the King, Queen and Princesses were entertained to a banquet in the City Hall, at which General Smuts made a moving speech, expressing the emotions of his people on first receiving their Sovereign in their midst, and the King replied with a simple address of thanks for the warmth of the popular welcome. The proceedings began and ended a good deal later than was set down in the programme, for the great parade ground outside the City Hall was densely packed with cheering people; it was a long slow process to clear a way for the royal car to the door, and even when they arrived the King and Queen were reluctant to go in to dinner until they had stood for some minutes on the balcony, waving smiling acknowledgments of the enthusiasm below. This again was to be a frequent experience all over the country; conscientious officials might work out their programmes to the minute, almost to the second, but they reckoned without the King and especially the Queen, and their steady refusal to forgo the exchange of friendly greetings with every section of their South African people who came to meet them on their path. Very late at night another slow and impeded drive through cheering crowds, while

brilliant illuminations of many colours shone down from every building upon the royal car, and a glimmering ghost of Table Mountain, floodlit by searchlights, towered over the city in the moonless dark, ended a day that had been consecrated to placing the Sovereign in formal relation with the principal personages representing the Union of South Africa as a whole.

On the second day the royal attention was turned to the affairs and personalities of the Cape Province and of the city of Cape Town. The first of many great popular gatherings was held on the parade ground which is the historic centre of the city. It is a broad open space, dominated on the south by the towering cliffs of Table Mountain, under which the not very impressive nineteenth-century architecture of the City Hall is dwarfed into insignificance. But at the eastern end the battlements of the Castle breathe the romance of three centuries of South African history; and opposite the fine vertical lines of the General Post Office suggest the expanding future that undoubtedly lies before a city which in the new age must be more than ever a centre of the traffic of the southern world. The motto of Cape Town, "Spes Bona" (Good Hope) was prominently displayed for the royal occasion on the façade of the City Hall, and seemed as full of significant meaning as ever it had been. The fourth side of the quadrilateral at one time abutted on the sea; but owing to recent works of land reclamation is now separated from the harbour's edge by some hundreds of yards of flat ground on which no doubt great new buildings will before long be erected.

Here on the morning of February 18 many thousands of people had assembled to fill the seats with which the parade had been covered, and thousands more were standing round the perimeter. On a platform facing the City Hall were not only the municipal dignitaries of Cape Town, but the mayors of many of the towns round about through which it had been found impossible to arrange that the Royal Family should pass on their coming journey. The royal party arrived amid cheers, and took their places on the platform, while the two national anthems were played. There followed a ceremony which was to become the model for similar proceedings in scores of cities and towns throughout South Africa, although here in the capital of a province it was on a larger scale

With officers and ship's company on board the Vanguard

Durban: arrival at the City Hall

and more elaborate in detail than in lesser towns. There were two distinct communities to welcome the King and Queen into their midst. First to speak was the Hon. J. G. Carinus, who represents the King as head of the Government of the Cape Province, corresponding to the Governor of a Canadian Province or an Australian State, but by South African usage bearing the title of Admini-strator. Few men could be better qualified than Mr. Carinus to represent to the Royal Family the essential character of one outstandingly important section of their South African subjects. He is, and is very proud to be, a typical Boer farmer, speaking little English, living the simplest life and cleaving fast to the old homely traditions of his people, persuaded to leave his farm temporarily and enter public life only by the sense of duty which is one of the greatest of those traditions. His short speech of welcome, though delivered in a language with which he was unfamiliar, was a direct and unaffected expression of the natural hospitality of the Afrikaner people, and suffered nothing by contrast with the more studied oratory of the Mayor of Cape Town, who followed him.

But in a different style Mr. Bloomberg delivered an address which will long be remembered by all who heard it for the resonant dignity of the utterance and the moving sincerity of the loyalty he expressed. He dwelt with admiration upon the qualities that the Royal Family had displayed during the war, on the inspiring leadership of the King and Queen, and especially upon their courage in remaining always close to the scene of danger during the darkest hours of the great aerial bombardment. From the storm of applause that greeted all these references it was apparent that here, in this record of endurance under fire, was one of the personal as opposed to the institutional aspects of the Royal Family which had already caught the imagination of the South African people. Again and again during the tour speakers would revert to this theme, and always they would draw an instant response from every kind of audience which showed that in all their movements during the beleaguered years the Royal Family had been watched from afar by the eyes of a great cloud of witnesses.

After the King had made a brief and happily phrased acknowledgment of the welcome, he stepped down from the platform with the Queen and Princesses to enter into conversation with a group of service men in hospital blue who had been given the front seats on the parade ground; then re-entering their car they drove off while the company, haltingly at first, then with increasing confidence, broke into the song, "For they are jolly good fellows." It seemed to mark another stage in the breaking down of barriers and the establishment of personal relations between Sovereign and people. That song, too, would become increasingly familiar as the Royal Family moved about the country.

Having thus been officially received in turn by the Nation, by the Province, and by the City, the Royal Family next devoted themselves to purely social pleasures. In the afternoon they attended a garden party in the beautiful terraced grounds of Westbrook, the official country house of the Governor General a few miles to the east of the city. Here many of the leading personalities of the neighbourhood who did not hold official positions were presented to the King and Queen, and many hundreds more had the opportunity of seeing them at close quarters as they walked up and down through the long avenues of guests. In the evening they attended a civic ball in the same room where the State dinner had been held the night before. So many invitations had been issued that dancing was practically impossible in the press, but this seemed to make no difference to the pleasure of the guests, who stood for hours in a solid mass, gazing fascinated at the faces of the royal party in a box above the dancing floor. Eventually, however, sufficient space was cleared for the two Princesses to come down and dance, Princess Elizabeth with the Mayor, and Princess Margaret with Mr. S. F. Waterson, Minister of Economic Development.

The third morning, by the King's personal desire, had been particularly set apart for the children of the Cape Peninsula. The programme provided for a drive out to the great naval base of Simonstown, and nearly all the way along the twenty miles of road the schools had lined up their thousands to cheer the procession as it passed. The first part of the journey lay through drab industrial streets; later on the road emerged into open country, and eventually it ran along the sea-shore through a succession of pleasant little white towns. But all the way there was the same rainbow

Oudtshoorn: clipping ostrich feathers

the bay; and once more the occasion seemed to be drawing together groups that history had set apart. Songs of welcome were sung by school choirs in three languages, English, Afrikaans, and Bantu; and of the nine little girls who carried up baskets of flowers to lay at the feet of the royal ladies, two were daughters of Admiral Moody, Commander-in-Chief, South Atlantic, and the others were drawn from the Afrikaner, Indian, Bantu, and Cape Coloured races. This was the first of many pretty little ceremonies of the same kind; and the nine pioneers set their successors a high standard by the grace of their curtsies and the ease and dignity with which they withdrew backwards from the royal presence.

Simonstown, the name of which commemorates Simon van der Stel, the successor of Van Riebeek, and perhaps the most distinguished of the Dutch Governors of the Cape, has been since the eighteenth century the chief naval harbour of South Africa and the prize for which the maritime Powers contended from the war of the Spanish Succession until the downfall of Napoleon lodged it finally in British hands. It is still a key point of imperial defence. At Admiralty House the King met naval officers from the United Kingdom as well as those of the South African Naval Force. This Force is indeed at present very small, and its commanders at least can be under no illusions that while it remains at its present strength the South African nation, which is the child of sea power, could exist in the bleak climate of the modern world as the independent republic that the extreme Nationalists claim. To a detached eye it would seem that the indispensable preliminary to the establishment of such a republic would be the building of a fleet many times as great as that which South Africa now possesses; but since the officers and men of the South African Naval Forces are strong royalists to a man, the strategic dilemma inherent in the republican argument seems to be insoluble.

pattern of boys and girls in red, green or blue uniforms, marshalled by the wayside and palpitating with excitement. Here, perhaps more significantly than on any occasion of the first two days, there was exposed to the royal gaze an indication of the fundamental problem of the country; for it was impossible not to notice that nearly everywhere European were ranged aloof from coloured and native schools, generally on opposite sides of the road. Here was the new generation still growing up into three communities and not one; the building of a nation, as a nation is understood in the Old World, was still only in an elementary stage. Yet with all the lines of cleavage that separate these various kinds of South Africans, it was also to be observed that they were all waving the same flag—for here in the Cape Peninsula the Union Jacks vastly outnumbered the Tricolours— they all had the same holiday grin on their faces, and they were all shouting in unison for the same King. If the dividing lines in South Africa go deep, the reconciling appeal of royalty goes deeper still.

The children were still in the forefront when the procession entered Simonstown to a salute of guns fired from ships of the Union Navy lying in

By this time the Royal Family had been engaged

Basutoland: on the way to the Pitso

almost incessantly for two and a half days in a strenuous round of official and semi-official functions—all of them happy experiences, no doubt, for they were laying the foundations of new friendships all the time, but some relaxation had been abundantly earned. So they went to seek it on the racecourse at Kenilworth, where the Queen and the Princesses put their money on the favourite in the Cape Town Derby and won their bets; and they finished the afternoon by a visit to the Joint Parliamentary Sports Meeting at Fernwood, where the Queen tried her luck in the old Afrikaner game of *Jukskei*. In the evening they made what was intended to be a flying visit to the ball given in the City Hall for the coloured community, but were so fascinated by the folk singing of three little Malay girls, and by the representation on the stage of a Malay wedding of the middle of the last century, that they stayed on long after their intended time of departure. Leading representatives of the coloured community were invited up to the royal box and given

Port Elizabeth: Johannes of the Snake Park

a most gracious reception. Many visitors from England who looked down upon the lively round dances below left with the impression that these coloured folk were an ebulliently cheerful people, who managed their entertainment with better organization and took their pleasures far more gaily than their European compatriots the night before. International publicists who declare in the assemblies of the world that this is an oppressed and miserable people would have got no support from the coloured ball.

Thursday, February 20, was the first day the royal party had spent in genuinely rural surroundings. They drove up the valleys of the Drakenstein Mountains, which radiate their gaunt ranges inland from the Cape Peninsula, in order to visit the wine-growing towns of Paarl and Stellenbosch. The drive showed them something of the hardship that the country had been suffering through prolonged drought, for the vines were scorched and yellow, and in many places forest fires were sending up smoke from the tinder-dry hillsides. Paarl, which is named after a smooth rocky hill near by that resembled a pearl in the eyes of the first settlers, is one of the oldest of the inland towns of the Cape Province, having been founded as far back as 1687 by a party of free burghers from Cape Town, who were later reinforced by French Huguenots, taking refuge in South Africa after the revocation of the Edict of Nantes. The presentation of local worthies, not only from Paarl but from all the villages round about, took place in a pleasant courtyard outside the town hall, shaded by oak trees; and some amusement was caused when the springing up of a sudden breeze caused the Royal Family to be bombarded with acorns. Many ex-service men and women, some of the former crippled by severe wounds, were lined up in ranks or lying in wheeled chairs round about the royal platform, and the King and Queen spent some time in friendly conversation with them before resuming the drive.

Their hosts then carried them off through some magnificent mountain scenery, enhanced by striking effects of changing light and shade as the sun appeared and disappeared behind rolling clouds, to a point near the summit of the Paarl Rock itself, commanding a noble view across the valley to the Drakenstein. Here, King, Queen and Princesses made acquaintance for the first time with the

At Graaff-Reinet

characteristic South African institution of the morning tea-party, which all over the Union was to be offered to them round about half-past eleven. Although generally described as light refreshment, these pleasant entertainments would by the standards of rationed England rank as quite a substantial meal. The wine growers of Paarl gave the party luncheon in the open air at the Government Experimental Fruit Farm at Bien Donné; and in the afternoon a ceremony on the same lines as that of the morning was held at the village of Stellenbosch. This name, which like that of Simonstown preserves the memory of Simon van der Stel, belongs to the oldest village in South Africa, where settled in 1679 the first European community to venture away from the sea coast of the peninsula. It is probably the most purely Afrikaner village in the Cape Province, and has the reputation of being strongly republican in sentiment. Certainly, although the people of Stellenbosch had turned out in force to meet the Royal Family, the reception here was in marked contrast with the demonstrative welcome at Paarl. No Union Jacks were visible, and the crowd for the most part received their visitors in a silence that was respectful but, to ears attuned to the cheers of Cape Town,

somewhat enigmatic. There was nothing hostile, and when the Royal Family left the town hall after the presentations there were some signs of an increasing friendliness in the demeanour of the crowd. But a reminder had been given that opposition to the idea of monarchy is a principle held with conviction by a substantial section of the South African people; and though their courtesy towards their royal visitors was never to falter at any time of the tour, they would not be easily carried away by any merely sentimental enthusiasm.

Behind the scenes that evening, when the King and Queen dined privately with General Smuts, there occurred a pleasant little episode of royal thoughtfulness. During the Boer War there had fallen into the hands of General Sir Horace Smith-Dorrien the family Bible of President Paul Kruger. The General's widow had placed this relic in the hands of the Queen, and after dinner the Queen gave it to the Prime Minister with the request that he would arrange for it to be returned after nearly half a century to the President's descendants.

Last and most significant of the state ceremonies in Cape Town was the ceremonial opening of the

Maseru: arrival of the Royal party at the Pitso

in attendance." This personal staff of private secretaries, ladies in waiting and equerries, numbered ten in all. One whole coach in the rear of the train, with its own dining-room and kitchen, was reserved for the Minister in Attendance; for, as in England, constitutional custom required a member of the Cabinet to be always with the King on his travels, ready to tender him advice, which would carry the authority of the whole Government, on every political problem that might arise. It goes without saying that while in South Africa the King was guided in all things by the advice of his South African Ministers, and that no member of the staff he had brought with him from overseas had any political connexion with the Government in the United Kingdom. He was, however, in constant touch with Whitehall, and indeed with all his Governments in the British Com-

East London: Leaving H.M.S.A.S. *Transvaal*

programme of the tour required to be continually available.

When all these indispensable assistants had been provided with their cabins, their offices, and their dining cars, it was not surprising that the White Train was the longest and heaviest that had ever traversed the South African railway system. It was, in fact, no less than a third of a mile long. Painted in ivory and gold, and constantly washed down by an army of cleaners who descended upon it with buckets and mops the moment it stopped at any of its staging points, its serpentine length was always a conspicuous and elegant addition to the landscape; and even when the Royal Family were known to have left it, parties of sightseers used regularly to come down from the towns outside which it halted, merely to gaze at its glistening exterior.

monwealth; and for this purpose a staff of cipher experts accompanied him on the train to send and receive the confidential messages that were passing daily between him and his four Prime Ministers outside South Africa. There were also a number of officials from South African Government departments; a manager of the royal tour with his staff; the Commissioner of Police, Major-General R. J. Palmer, with several officers of lower rank; a body of railway officials; catering managers, electricians, personal servants, and other persons whom the elaborate

Long as it was, the White Train alone could not accommodate all the people who were required to accompany the tour. All the way round the Union it was preceded, half an hour ahead, by a "Pilot Train," in which travelled the rank and file of the police and railway representatives, the newspaper correspondents and photographers, and such individual artists as the King's barber and the supervisor of the flowers in the royal apartments. There was, corresponding to the Minister's coach on the White Train, a coach which was occupied by the Administrator of the Province through

Bonza Beach, East London

Port Elizabeth: the garden party in Victoria Park

which the tour was passing at the time, with room for his secretary and, if he chose, his wife and family. To the Pilot Train also was allotted the important function of keeping the whole expedition in touch with the outside world. It had a post office coach, a telegraph office, and even wireless communication with the White Train and with the general international system, for use while the two trains were in motion. Both trains had telephone circuits along their whole length, by which passengers could communicate with one another; and directly they stopped these were

The three trains, however, were not in themselves by any means sufficient to cover all the needs of the royal transport. A fleet of thirteen or fourteen large motor cars accompanied the party everywhere, meeting the trains at every stopping point, ready to drive the royal party, the household, the police, officials, and even the press round every town to be visited. In many cases these towns might lie fifty or sixty miles from the railway line. Sometimes passengers from the Pilot Train, who had to follow the royal party, could not get back to the station before their own train left; and it

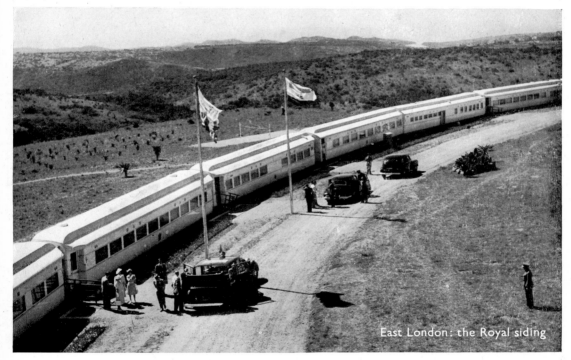

East London: the Royal siding

connected up to the national system, and so, if necessary, to countries overseas. The King, in fact, spoke frequently during the tour to his brother, the Duke of Gloucester, who was acting as first of the Counsellors of State in England; and at any time required his Ministers in Great Britain and the other Dominions were able to consult him personally. Princess Elizabeth, also, sometimes spoke to Mr. Philip Mountbatten.

The railway cortège was completed by a third train, popularly known as "The Ghost Train," which followed several hours behind the White Train and carried spare parts, and repairing gear for the railway service.

was necessary for these to be driven at high speed for a hundred miles or more in order to catch up. When it is added that the cars, in addition to the long detours they made away from the railway line, had themselves to keep up continuously with trains that were maintaining an average of at least two hundred miles in every twenty-four hours, and that consequently they had often to travel most of the night, it will be appreciated that their devoted drivers, who carried on throughout the tour without a relief, rank by no means lowest among those who contributed to the success of the royal visit.

There was one other transport organization. The King's Flight of four Viking aircraft, under the command of its Captain, Air Commodore Fielden, had flown out from England in advance of the *Vanguard,* and was always ready to carry the royal party on occasions when the distance to be travelled was too long and the time too short for the train to fulfil their needs.

In Cape Town, with the half-million inhabitants of the city and its satellites crowding to watch the royal progresses, it had been difficult to understand how a country eight or nine times the size of the United Kingdom could have less than a quarter of its population. As the train emerged from the Cape Peninsula at Paarl, its passengers began to see the other side of the picture. The journey lay through a hilly country covered with

In the Natal National Park

to feel intolerably shut in, and goes on trek. Yet although there was scarcely a building to be seen anywhere, in little groups of two or three beside the line, with a ramshackle car or a few tethered donkeys behind them, the sparse inhabitants of this almost empty land had come down to stand and watch the royal train steam by. Many of these people had probably ridden or driven fifty miles to keep this unwritten assignation with their Sovereign. They knew that they had not a hundred-to-one chance of even seeing a royal face at the window; but they had come apparently for the sake of being for once in their lives close to the royal presence. They were of all races, English, Dutch, Native, and Coloured. To

low scrub, a country indeed more productive than it looked, for it nourishes vast flocks of sheep, but one in which for mile after mile there was never a visible sign of human habitation. Here one began to understand the old saying that when a Boer farmer sees smoke arising from a neighbour's chimney on the farthest horizon he begins the seeing eye there was a loyalty here that was certainly not less moving than any that could be proclaimed by the cheering crowds of the great cities; and the same thing was to repeat itself in the lonely places all along the route of the royal tour.

February 21. In as lonely a place as any the royal train came to a halt that night, where the first of

At Pietermaritzburg

many special sidings, with water supply, telephone lines, and lighting laid on, had been prepared for the occasion by the State Railway authorities. It lay in a vineyard close to the Breede River, and before departing in the morning the Royal Family walked over to the farm house of the vine-grower, Meneer van der Merwe, to thank him for his hospitality, drink coffee with him, and taste his wines.

February 22. But the day was still young when the train was in motion again, and by ten o'clock it had arrived at Worcester, the centre of the great fruit-growing area of Boland, standing in the midst of thousands of acres of grapes, peaches, apricots, and plums. Worcester is a town of nineteen thousand inhabitants, founded in 1818 by settlers under the authority of Lord Charles Somerset, then Governor of the Cape, and named by him after the marquessate of Worcester, the second of the peerages held by his family, the Dukes of Beaufort. The Royal Family had just an hour to spend there, and they spent it in a way that would become a matter of routine in most of the towns of moderate size that they were to visit on their long journey. But although from their own point of view these receptions by their rural subjects, or at least the formal part of the receptions, were bound to become an affair of endless repetition, they never forgot that for their hosts at each stopping place this was a unique occasion, to be remembered and talked about perhaps for years afterwards. The King would leave every local dignitary feeling that a special personal interest had been taken in him; the warmth of the Queen's accents and the kindliness of her smile would never be impaired, and would go straight to each individual heart.

At Worcester, as it would be elsewhere, the Mayor, accompanied by his town council and municipal dignitaries from places lying remote from the railway line, was waiting on the platform for the train to arrive. Directly it came to a standstill—and everywhere the careful calculations of the railway staff and the skill of the driver managed to halt it so that the door of the royal compartment precisely coincided with the beginning of the red carpet—the King, Queen and Princesses appeared at the entrance and the local band played the two national anthems while the King acknowledged the salute. Then the Minister in Attendance—at Worcester it was Mr. F. C. Sturrock, Minister of Transport—presented the Mayor and the local member of the House of Assembly. Worcester also returns a member to the Council of the Province, so he was presented by the Provincial Administrator, as were the mayors and mayoresses of half a dozen towns in the vicinity. Finally the Mayor presented the members of his own town council and his Town Clerk. All these people having filed before the members of the Royal Family and made their formal bows or curtsies to each, the group dissolved in a few minutes into easy conversation before the drive round the town began.

The object of the drive, and many another drive in subsequent weeks, was to allow every possible man, woman, and child to enjoy the sight of the Royal Family; and on this first occasion the purpose was very abundantly achieved, for Worcester is a town of low buildings and broad, straight streets laid out in the pattern of a chess board. The length of the street fronts in proportion to the number of houses is very great, so that not only could the crowds spread themselves thinly along the route, but the more athletic, by leaping across the broad gardens from one street to the next parallel, could meet the procession several times as the royal car drove slowly up, down, and across. There were many large parties from schools, both white and coloured, and stops were made at a European school for the blind, and a school for the coloured deaf. The passage from the cheering streets to the dead silence within the precincts of this latter institution had an eerie effect; but the flags were waving with double enthusiasm to compensate for the lack of audible expression of loyalty. Within the hour from the moment of arrival the Royal Family were back at the railway station, the Mayor and Mayoress had said good-bye on behalf of the town, and the train was off on its way to George.

Although each place visited had naturally its own special characteristics, requiring this or that variation of the standard programme, this reception at Worcester and drive round the town show the structural skeleton on which every visit of this duration was to be based.

Some places, of course, could not be given even so much as one hour of the royal attention; and at many of these the best that could be done was for all the people to come down to the station, where they were formed up on the platform to watch the

A Zulu dancer at Eshowe

Inspection at Bloemfontein

train pass. At most of these stations the train halted at least for five or ten minutes, and when it did the King and Queen very seldom failed to come out and walk along the ranks, pausing here and there to ask a question of one of the citizens, especially men and women wearing the medals of the South African or later wars, or the Springbok button of the Union's ex-service men. There were several stations on the way to George at which this procedure was followed, including one for which no stop was scheduled in the programme. This was Swellendam, which has the reputation of being one of the great strongholds of the Nationalist Party. Swellendam's political idiosyncrasy is very ancient; it declared itself an independent republic as long ago as 1795, when its burghers, under the influence of the French Revolution, rebelled against the Dutch East India Company. It is now represented in Parliament by Mr. Warren, one of the most irreconcilable Republicans. But in response to a telegram from the Mayor the King ordered the train to stop, and found himself and his family greeted as warmly by a crowd that filled the station as they had been at any town through which they had yet passed.

From Swellendam the line, which here is crossing a broad peninsula under the shadow of the Langesberge Mountains on its left, runs down to the sea, which it reaches at Mossel Bay. Darkness had fallen by the time it arrived here, and the further journey to George made it too late for an official entry into the town to be considered that night.

February 23. This was the end of the first week spent by the Royal Family in South Africa; and according to an arrangement which was faithfully observed throughout the tour, they had asked to have their Sunday in privacy. They did not go into the town. Accompanied only by the members of the household, the Minister in Attendance (Mr. Sturrock), and one or two distinguished local residents, they drove out through the picturesque area called The Wilderness to Ebb and Flow, at the mouth of the Touw River, where the Bishop of George held an open-air service for them. The rest of the day was devoted to a picnic and a walk through the woods, and Their Majesties made their first acquaintance with the South African *braaivleis*, which is an open-air meal at which meats are grilled on braziers over a wood fire. The

principal dishes were *sasaties*—slices of mutton pickled in curry and skewered on little sticks— and *boerevors*, which is the Afrikaans for farmer's sausages.

February 24. Nowhere more than in this south-western region of the Cape Province are English and Afrikaner communities to be found alternating. Swellendam had been overwhelmingly Dutch; the little cathedral city of George is probably more English than any small town in the Union. It is the only place in Africa where hops are grown— a peculiarity that it owes to its damp climate. Lying close to the sea and surrounded by mountains and forests, it is a place of picturesque beauty which Anthony Trollope in 1877 described as "the prettiest village in the world—at least the prettiest I have ever seen." It was the first town founded after the Cape came into British possession, and its early history is dominated by the bizarre figure of George Rex, who, according to a persistent but improbable legend, was the son of King George III and Hannah Lightfoot the Quakeress. Rex was sent out to Africa by Pitt's Government, to whom his presence in England had become an increasing embarrassment, in 1796. He went with considerable pomp under the escort of an Admiral of the Royal Navy, and was allowed to give himself decidedly royal airs in the Colony, provided he did not again raise the blushes of the Royal Family by returning to England. His adventures fill a respectable chapter in early colonial history, and he left numerous progeny, some of whom were able to entertain Queen Victoria's son, Alfred, Duke of Edinburgh, when he visited the Cape Colony in 1860.

The postponed visit to George took place on Monday morning, and lasted an hour and a half. It followed much the same lines as that to Worcester, except that most of the presentations were made, not at the railway station, but in the town's Garden of Remembrance, where a platform had been erected, and a large assembly had gathered to watch the proceedings. The Town Council had prepared an address of welcome, but by a convenient arrangement which was continued throughout the tour except in capitals of provinces and other cities of outstanding importance, this was presented in writing by the Mayor, and the King handed a written reply. These expressions of municipal loyalty are by no means to be undervalued;

they are placed on record, and serve in after years to remind the townspeople of the significance of the royal visit. But inevitably they must follow stereotyped lines; if spoken, they take time to deliver, and the more the proceedings at each town can be curtailed without the omission of essentials, the greater the number of towns that can be given a sight of the Royal Family in their streets.

An almost identical ceremonial was performed in the afternoon at Oudtshoorn, after a journey through magnificent mountain scenery, winding up over the Monatagu Pass to cross the Outeniqua Range.

At Power, the first stop on the way up to the pass, occurred an incident that was both amusing and touching. An elderly Boer farmer, who had seen the Royal Family at George, had galloped alongside the train on his Basuto pony, and now arrived panting at Power railway station, determined to get another sight of them. He was brought up and presented to the King, who tactfully drew from

Dignitaries of Basutoland

Left to right: High Commissioner for Basutoland, Sir Evelyn Baring, K.C.M.G.; The resident Commissioner, Lt.-Col. A. D. Forsyth Thompson, C.M.G., C.B.E.; The Regent of Basutoland, Paramount Chieftainess Mantsebo Seeiso, and her interpreter.

him a good deal of his life's history. His name was Henry Dreyer, and he had fought for the republics in the South African War. He had been out again with the rebels in 1914, and his sentiments had remained Nationalist ever since. But the actual sight of his King and Queen at George had converted him and won his heart. The King asked him what was the story of the remarkable belt that he was wearing, and Mr. Dreyer explained that it was an outstanding specimen of the native workmanship of an obscure central African tribe. It had been his particular treasure for more than thirty years, and he was still dilating on its beauties when the train moved off. He hesitated

for a moment; then, tearing off the belt, he ran along the platform and handed it through the window to Wing-Commander Townsend, the King's Equerry, saying, "Here, give it to him." At Camper, the next halt, an old man asked that Princess Elizabeth might look in the direction of his son, who was an invalid in a car and could not be moved; the car was behind the crowd, in the rear of the platform. The Queen, when she heard of it, had the barrier lowered, and took the Princesses over to the boy, whose name was Clive Taube. The father was so overwhelmed with gratitude that he broke down.

Oudtshoorn is famous as the centre of the ostrich feather industry, and all the members of the Royal Family had looked forward to the visit that had been arranged to an ostrich farm at Le Roux, a few miles beyond the town. The industry, owing to changes of fashion, has not of late enjoyed the abounding prosperity of a generation ago; but the Queen, who is well aware of its importance to South Africa, had paid it the compliment of wearing ostrich feathers for her landing from the *Vanguard*, and on many occasions during the tour she used them to ornament her dresses or carried them in the shape of a fan. They had formed a conspicuous part of the decoration of the City Hall at Cape Town for the series of State functions that had been held there in the first week of the visit. Now the Royal Family came to the farm of Mr. Meyers to see the "primary producers." They spent some time gazing fascinated at fifty or sixty of the strange stately birds, which gazed back with the fixed and slightly contemptuous stare that is their permanent expression and takes no account of human royalty. By special request of Princess Margaret, a family of ostrich chicks a month old were on show in a separate pen, and caused much amusement by the incongruous combination of the fluffiness of extreme youth with a haughtiness of demeanour scarcely to be surpassed by their parents. Before leaving the farm, each member of the Royal Family accepted their host's invitation to cut the feathers of his or her choice from the tails of some of the finest of the young cock ostriches.

into country full of historic memories of the long, arduous and bitter struggle that raged about the turn of the eighteenth and nineteenth centuries between the white settlers, pushing out eastward, and the native tribes, feeling their way south under pressure from still more ferocious peoples in their rear. The first place visited on Tuesday, February 25, was Graaff-Reinet, which in its day was the last outpost of the Dutch colony, and after the manner of outposts felt itself

Matsieng village: home of the Paramount Chieftainess

At Suyberg, where the train stopped for a few minutes at dusk, the station was crowded with native children, who were singing songs of their own people in a slow and haunting rhythm. This was the Royal Family's first experience of the natural harmonic singing of the Bantu peoples, which was to greet them often as they passed through the smaller stations of the Eastern Cape Province. The train finally halted for the night at another specially constructed siding, which had been given the happily romantic name of Koningsrust, or King's Rest.

February 25. Next morning the train moved

misunderstood and ill supported by headquarters. Its story is the story of the French Revolution in Africa. While Cape Town became fascinated by one aspect of Rousseau's theories, the doctrine of the noble savage, the men of Graaff-Reinet, who were in actual daily contact with the savage on the border, and had their own ideas about his nobility, raised the standard of "liberty, equality, fraternity," and proclaimed an independent republic. This was in 1795, just a week before the first English squadron anchored in Table Bay. The result was that, after Cape Town had submitted, the republic of Graaff-

Reinet, which had come into existence by rebellion against the Dutch, remained for another year in a sort of derivative rebellion against their British supplanters. The dangers of Kaffir wars, however, eventually forced them to make common cause with the new masters. To-day, Graaff-Reinet is one of the principal stock-raising districts of the Cape Midlands; and it gave the Royal Family one of the warmest welcomes they had yet received, with Union Jacks waving everywhere and a town hall decked with flowers which, even in a land of flowers, remained memorable as among the finest of all such displays during the tour.

February 26. So the train moved on, over land where the map is spotted with the names of half-forgotten battles between white man and black, to the harbour of Port Elizabeth. What is now a great industrial town, with a population of a hundred and fifty thousand, mainly engaged either in the service of the docks or in the manufacture of boots and shoes, confectionery, and motor accessories, was founded as a fortress during the Napoleonic wars, to protect the eastern frontier of the Cape against the danger, ever present before Trafalgar, of a French landing. Its original name of Fort Frederick commemorated an old alliance; but Lord Charles Somerset, who chose it as the landing place for the 1820 settlers, rechristened it by the name of his dead wife. The memory of the settlers is still the pride of Port Elizabeth, and their tall monument, in which is hung the carillon of bells commemorating King George V, dominates the town.

Outstanding among the entertainments that the loyalty of Port Elizabeth offered to the Royal Family were the great gatherings of children who received them in St. George's Park. In the middle of the park the usual ceremony was enacted; the Mayor delivered the usual address in writing, and in writing received the royal reply. The eminent personages of the town were presented, and the royal visitors signed the golden book. But probably Mayor and Councillors would be the first to acknowledge that these dignified formalities took second place to the rapturous demonstration accorded by the eighteen thousand European school children who packed the stands all round the great area of the Crusader Ground. The welcome by the children of Port Elizabeth was to mark an epoch

in the tour; it set a standard that other towns farther along the route strained themselves to emulate or surpass; but, although bigger centres of population might produce a larger muster, nothing ever excelled the freshness and spontaneity of this great welcome. The children had been in their places since half-past six in the morning, and the Royal Family did not arrive until nearly eleven. But their enthusiasm never flagged for a moment. For hour after hour they sat and cheered everybody and everything—the Mayor, the Councillors, every minor official attending to details of preparation, and especially the troop of young girls in plaids and kilts who entertained them with highland dances while they waited. Here was a reminder of the great part that Scottish pioneers played in the stern adventure of the 1820 settlement; the ancient Royal Banner of Scotland, displayed in Port Elizabeth almost as prominently as the Union Jack, was another, and there would be many more such reminders as the tour progressed. For since 1820 the Scots have penetrated deep into every Province of the Union, and to this day half its famous regiments march to the music of pipe bands, arrayed in the tartans of the Highland clans. The Queen especially, seeking out in conversation these heirs of the tradition of her native country, was to find that hearts still thrilled to the old allegiance after several generations under the Southern Cross.

But those eighteen thousand children were of every stock that has gone to the making of South Africa: English, Scottish, Dutch, and even German, for in this region there are descendants of the Prussian immigrants who were offered a home in Cape Colony and landed at East London after fighting with the British Army in the Crimean War. When the Royal Family arrived the uproar seemed to be lifting the roof off the stands, and it was several minutes before the band could make the two national anthems heard. When at last they could be played, it was noteworthy that the children, predominantly English-speaking though they were, sang "Die Stem" as lustily as "God Save the King"; and, since in the towns previously visited the Afrikaans-speakers had seemed curiously reluctant to lift up their voices in song, this was probably the first time the Royal Family had had the chance to appreciate the full choral value of their South African anthem.

The White Train near Umtata

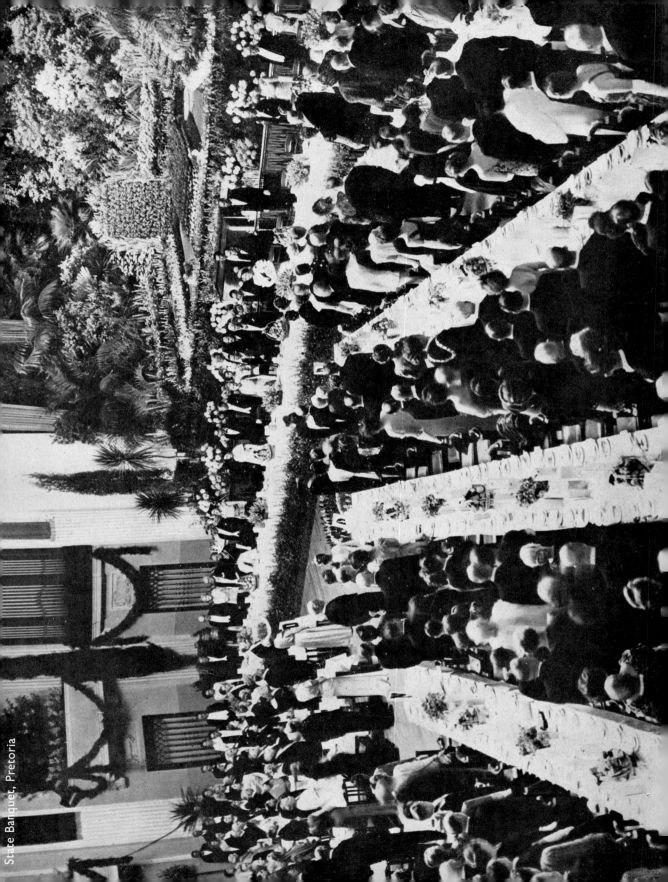

State Banquet, Pretoria

In the Drakensberg Mountains

February 27. This was only to be the first of two children's demonstrations; for the next morning St. George's Park was filled nearly as full with coloured children, who, with perhaps squeakier voices, rounder eyes and mouths, and a more uncontrollable tendency to wriggle and hop, sang and cheered with equal glee, and did their very best, despite their slight inferiority of numbers, to make as much noise as their white fellow-subjects.

In the afternoon the Royal Family performed one of their ceremonial drives through many miles of streets in the suburb of New Brighton, which is mainly inhabited by Xosa, Fingo, and other Bantu families, saw the solid and comfortable, though regrettably ugly, cottages provided on the municipal housing estates, waved their greetings back to the grinning dark faces that greeted them along every yard of the way, and were entertained here and there by singers, by dancers in ceremonial attire of lavish pipeclay and jingling shells, and by one solitary performer who wore the singular costume of a European waistcoat and trousers with a complete lion's skin in lieu of a coat. They went on to visit the special pride of Port Elizabeth, the Snake Park, where they watched fascinated as Johannes and Daniel, the coloured keepers, twisted dozens of the deadliest serpents in Africa into ropes and festoons about their arms, or tossed a sack full of puff adders carelessly about the sunken lawn at the royal feet.

The Royal Family spent forty-eight hours at Port Elizabeth, and in spite of a full programme of official engagements, which included a garden party and a fine parade of ex-service men as well as those already mentioned, found time to appreciate the reason why the town is famous as a holiday resort. The siding built for the White and Pilot trains was in a particularly charming position, actually on the shore; the Princesses were able to ride along the sands before breakfast, and the whole royal party tended to spend almost every free moment in the sea. Indeed, the King's effort to rescue and revive one of the ladies in waiting, who had pretended to be drowning, was so realistic that some of the newspaper correspondents had almost completed their sensational cables to London before the fictitious character of the drama was explained to them. It was with the happiest memories of a visit that had notably combined business with pleasure that the Royal Family and their entourage left Port Elizabeth on the morning of Friday, February 28.

Natal National Park

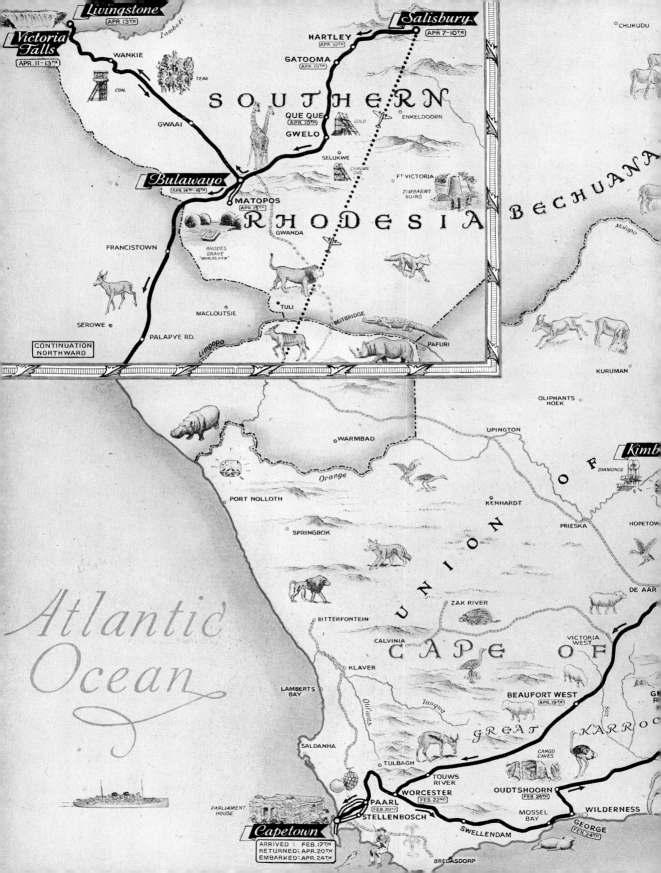

February 28. Early in the afternoon they left the train at Alicedale, and, after receiving the leaders of that little community, went on by road across the veld into the Cape Highlands, where Grahamstown nestles among wooded hills. It was founded by Colonel Thomas Graham, a distinguished officer of the frontier garrison, in 1812. Grahamstown has repeated the transformation of Oxford seven hundred years ago, and changed from a fortress to a place of learning. In its early days it was an outpost constantly besieged by savage tribes; it is now a cathedral city set about with schools and colleges. It has one of the four universities of the Union, and St. Andrew's College competes with Diocesan College, Rondebosch (familiarly known as Bishops) for the title of the principal public school in South Africa. The King paid graceful compliment to the academic distinction of the city in his speech replying to the Mayor's welcome; and although light rain had been falling in the middle of the day, the sun came out just in time to make the Grahamstown garden party one of the pleasantest of the tour. It was at Grahamstown, in the market square, where the native community was assembled, many of the mothers among them carrying their babies, like inverted kangaroos, in pouches of blanket strapped to their backs, that the King first heard himself hailed with the salute, "*A Sozizwe,*" meaning "Father of Nations."

As the train left Alicedale that evening, the Royal Family realized that they were journeying into a land of song. At the wayside stations, crowds of native men and women were pressing upon the ropes that held them back from the platform, and as the train steamed in they would break into the Bantu National Anthem, and continue with other songs of their own people. The simple melodies ascending in the moonlight created a charming and romantic effect, and at the little town of Cookhouse, where the Royal Family left the train for a few minutes to listen to the songs, the King was heard to remark to the Queen on the astonishing art of the singers. Many times afterwards they were to hear the Bantu national anthem, "*Nkosi sikelel'i Africa,*" or "Lord, bless Africa." Sung unaccompanied and in harmony, as it generally is, the tune makes its own haunting appeal to the heart; but to many hearers it seems always to carry the undertone of a chant by

the waters of Babylon, and to breathe the muted melancholy of a disinherited people.

March 1. Next morning the royal party heard the full musical performance of which these singings by the wayside were the charming and informal overture. Driving out from the little town of Alice they came to Lovedale, which was founded as a mission station in 1824 by Presbyterians from Scotland. One of the missionaries, Mr. Love, has left his name embodied in that of the town. Lovedale has been called "the black man's Eton and the black man's Oxford"; its schools, together with the South African native college at Fort Hare, a few miles away, are responsible for most of the higher education of natives of both sexes in the Cape Province. Those of undergraduate standing may read for degrees of the University of South Africa.

In a natural amphitheatre surrounded by low hills, five thousand boy and girl students were drawn up in ranks according to their colleges, and conducted by a Bantu professor, D. D. T. Jabavu. So vast a choir had never had the opportunity to practise together; they had met as a body for the first time early that same morning, and many of them had walked ten miles to the rendezvous. But their singing was of a quality that would have done credit to any concert hall. Besides the Bantu national anthem they sang a beautiful vernacular setting of the verses from Judges, Chapter v, beginning, "Awake, awake, Deborah," and a chant, "*Sele sele ahom ahom,*" which reproduces the sound of treble and tenor bells. Their soft and limpid harmonies, rising unaccompanied in the sunshine of an absolutely still morning, while big and gaudy butterflies flitted in and out among the royal party on the platform, will long be remembered by those who heard them as an epitome of the golden African summer which was now slowly declining towards autumn. After the songs the Royal Family spent more than half an hour walking in and out among the singers, the King especially entering into vivacious talk with many of them. The Bantu salute of "*A sozizwe*" followed him as the cars drove away.

The afternoon's journey, which was halted several times to allow the Royal Family to greet more parties of singers at the small stations, led down the valley of the Buffalo River to the harbour of East London. Throughout the last fifty miles the national road runs alongside the line, and hundreds

City Hall, Durban: the civic welcome

Eshowe: a Zulu dancer

Knysna, into the mouth of the Buffalo River—an event that caused the town in its earlier days to be called Port Rex—the estuary was blocked by sand and incapable of navigation. The history of East London has moved in rhythm with the gradual clearing and development of the channel, till now it is the one great river port of the Union, and is capable of receiving all the ocean-going vessels of the Union Castle Line. One much desired improvement, which had been projected for many years, had at last been undertaken under the stress of war. This was the construction of a graving dock, a formidable task, since the only possible site was the bed of a tributary to the Buffalo called the Gabbanga River, which had to be diverted from its course for the purpose. The work had been begun in 1944, and was completed in time for the South African railway authorities, which administer the harbours as well as the railways on behalf of the Government, to invite the Princess to perform the opening ceremony.

of motor cars fell into column along it to keep pace with the train. This impromptu escort conducted them all the way to the Cambridge station on the outskirts of the town, where they were received by a guard of honour of the Kaffrarian Rifles, and made a rapid circuit of the decorated streets. Apart, however, from an inspection of a parade of ex-service men and women, they postponed the main ceremonial until over the week-end.

March 3. The Monday was Princess Elizabeth's day. Hitherto she had been a demurely silent figure, walking or driving with her sister behind the King and Queen, cheered wherever she went, but scarcely emerging as a separate personality in the eyes of the South African people. Now at East London the Heiress Presumptive took the centre of the stage in her own right. A great event in the life of the town was to be celebrated. In the days when old George Rex sailed his brig, the

The open area round the dock was packed with people, who cheered lustily as, for the first time in South Africa, the Princess's own banner of arms was broken from a flagstaff over the platform on her arrival. There was a sense of eagerness in the air as people waited to make their appraisal of this new character in their national life; and the Princess seemed instinctively to respond to it. Though a brisk wind was blowing up from the sea, and she had constant difficulty in holding her hat in place with one hand and her skirt with the other, her speech came over the air clear-cut and confident, instinct with the hopefulness of youth; and it was the youth of a young country that led the applause. She spoke of the widening future that lay before the great harbour, and then, as she declared the dock open, naval ratings hoisted the signal "C," to indicate that the first ship might enter, and simultaneously at the dock head the veil fell from the naming stone, a simple obelisk on which the title "Princess Elizabeth Dock" was engraved in English and Afrikaans. As the Princess sat down Mrs. Sturrock, wife of the Minister of Transport, handed her, as a present from the Railways and Harbours Administration, a set of fine diamonds from the Government mines on the Orange River. Inadvertently the microphone had not been disconnected, and the Princess's spontaneous exclamation of delight, revealing that the dignified orator of a moment before was also an unaffected young girl, gave evident pleasure to the great audience.

Meanwhile the frigate H.M.S.A.S. *Transvaal* was steaming slowly towards the entrance of the dock. Bands on shore played her up stream with "Life on the Ocean Wave"; she broke a glass ribbon stretched across the dock mouth and came to her berth to the tune of "*Sarie Marais,*" one of the most characteristic of all South African songs, whose melody seems to have caught and distilled the sunshine and gaiety of the land. It was to

Eshowe: a Zulu survivor of Isandhlwana

become a special favourite with the King, who more than once called for an encore when it was played at banquets or other ceremonies. The Princess went on board the *Transvaal* to inspect the ship's company and meet the officers before returning to rejoin her mother, who had spent the morning visiting the town hospital. The Queen had not been present at the dock, and did not hear her daughter's fine performance until some weeks later, when it was reproduced as part of a film of the royal tour exhibited one evening outside the White Train. Those who were present observed that Her Majesty was quite unable to conceal the pride that any less exalted mother would have felt on a like occasion. A garden party and a civic ball completed the ceremonies of the day.

March 4. Before leaving East London next day, the King, Queen and Princesses found time to attend the parade of the British Empire Service League, which was holding its annual assembly in the town. This is a society organized on similar lines to the British Legion in the United Kingdom, but is open to women who have left the three services as well as to men. Two thousand delegates of both sexes marched past, marshalled in companies representing South Africa's three modern wars, those of 1899, 1914, and 1939; and they carried Colours which had been dedicated in Westminster Abbey in 1934 and 1938, when detachments from the Legion made pilgrimages to the European battlefields of the first world war.

In the afternoon the royal party resumed their journey by road, driving some forty miles up the valley of the Buffalo to Kingwilliamstown, once a fortress named after King William IV, and now the administrative centre for the natives of the area known as the Ciskei; after meeting many of the citizens at an open-air tea party and attending

Arriving for the Durban Ball

a native gathering a few miles out of the town, they went on across the Kei River into the Transkei, which was formerly known as Kaffirland.

March 5. Here, next morning, they found themselves for the first time in a district reserved for native occupation, in which no European may reside without a special permit. It is a part of old Africa still surviving, where justice is administered according to tribal custom, where the people live in kraals, each made up of perhaps a dozen round thatched huts, and where the agricultural work in the mealie fields, from which the community derives its food, is left entirely to the women. The men, on the other hand, may travel far afield and enter into industrial employment in many parts of the Union, returning with the money they have earned to the reservation at the end of the season's work.

On a space of open downland in the midst of the rolling hills were assembled some fifteen thousand natives, who had come from all parts of the Transkei, some of them travelling as far as a hundred miles, to greet their King. All were men, for this is a land where the sexes are invariably segregated on ceremonial occasions, and the women had played their part in the welcome by assembling along the road from the capital town of Umtata to

cheer the royal procession as it passed. The King, setting a precedent which he followed at all similar native assemblies, appeared on the platform in the white uniform of an Admiral of the Fleet, with the blue ribbon of the Garter across his breast and a gold-hilted sword at his side. In order to throw his figure into greater prominence it became the custom that none of his staff except a single equerry should wear uniform. Although there were some who held that in appearing before a simple-minded people it would have been appropriate for the King to wear some more spectacular robes, there is no doubt that the simple dignity of white and gold, gleaming in the African sun and contrasting with the bright colours affected by many of the native potentates who did him homage, made him stand out as pre-eminently the chief above all chiefs.

To a European eye seeking the picturesque, the attire of the natives themselves at these ceremonial gatherings was a great deal less happy. On the roads around Umtata, or working in the fields, both men and women had been seen wearing with a fine freedom and grace the saffron-dyed blanket which is the traditional dress of the Transkei. But they had refused to appear thus

The Queen with the Mayor of Durban

At the special request of the King, Mr. Cornelius Mostert's height was measured—7 ft. 3 ins.

before the King, "lest His Majesty should think we are naked savages." So the whole of the great Umtata gathering were dressed in European lounge suits, most of them, it could not but be observed, far from accurately fitting, and in many cases the magnificent sinews of an athletic race threatening to disrupt the workmanship of the cheap tailors of Cape Town. But if there was a good deal that was incongruous in the individual figures, there was also a sense of solidity and discipline about the whole great array which added force to their evident loyalty. Chief Jeremiah Moshesh, who delivered in English the address of welcome, spoke with sonorous eloquence, and after the King's reply, which dwelt upon the war service of the people, and gave them fatherly advice on husbandry, had been translated into Xosa, the royal procession left

to the booming accompaniment of the Bantu salute, the famous triple "*Bayete.*"

Late that night, as the White Train halted at a minor station, bad news cast sadness over the conclusion of the tour of the Cape Province. A message was received that the "Ghost Train" had been derailed some hours before, and that the driver had been severely injured. In the morning it became known that he had died of his injuries. The King and Queen were deeply distressed, and sent a message of sympathy to his family.

March 6. With brief visits of an hour each to the frontier towns of Queenstown and Aliwal North, leaving time for the usual presentations and drive round the streets, the Royal Family said good-bye to the Cape Province. Their reception throughout its length had surpassed in enthusiasm even the high expectations of Mr. Carinus, the Administrator, who now took leave of them until they should re-enter the Province in the last days of the tour. Far more people than he had dared to prophesy had found the means of placing themselves at one point or another upon the royal route, and the depth of their loyalty was shown by the real sacrifice that many of them had had to make in order to do so. As has so often been the experience of England, and as it had been just before the war in Canada and the United States, it had been above all the graciousness and warm-hearted friendliness of the Queen that had first captured the people's imagination. Those who had come into personal contact, even if only for a moment, with the Royal Family had, however, perceived that an equal responsiveness to the thoughts and feelings of ordinary people radiated from the King; and the awe attaching to his great office, which at first had tended to obscure his personality, was now beginning to blend with, and be enriched by, the recognition that this was a man of the widest human sympathies, devoting a laborious life to the furtherance of his subjects' welfare. More and more this conception of the King's personality was beginning to find expression in the South African papers, which in this matter undoubtedly reflected the feelings of their readers. As for the native peoples, the excitement of standing at last in the presence of the almost legendary potentate to whom they had so long looked up as the embodiment of the power and glory of the world made

In Mitchell Park, Durban

the day of his passing across their vision the most solemn of each man's life. They were apt to express their sense of its transcendent magnificence, as they did at Umtata, by holding a mighty nocturnal feast or *braaivleis*, for which three hundred head of cattle were slaughtered.

THE ORANGE FREE STATE AND BASUTOLAND

A FEW miles beyond Aliwal North the White Train crossed the Orange River, which separates the Cape Province from the Orange Free State. It was moving in the trail of the hunters of 1828, who first crossed from the Cape to explore the great central tableland of what is now the Union. They were followed in 1836 by one of the main bodies of the Voortrekkers under A. H. Potgieter, who established the first republic with its centre at Bloemfontein. In 1846 Sir Harry Smith, Governor of the Cape, claiming the rights of sovereignty over the trekkers, annexed the country; but the Coalition Government of Lord Aberdeen was persuaded to restore its independence, and in 1854 J. P. Hoffman took office as first President of a republic that was to last until 1902. As has been stated earlier, the Orange Free State, after fighting on the losing side in the South African War, was brought back under the British Crown as the Orange River Colony; but in a very few years its name and its rights of self-government were restored, and it entered the Union as an equal partner in 1910. One of its most distinguished citizens, General Hertzog,

became the second Prime Minister of the Union, first in opposition to General Smuts, his brother officer in the South African War, and eventually in coalition with him.

The Free State is to-day very much what it has always been, a province of big farms, in which industrialism has made less mark than anywhere else in the Union. Whether the very recent discovery of rich deposits of gold within its boundaries will change its economic structure and the social character of its people, is one of the great questions of the immediate South African future. Hitherto the men and women of the Free State have been a community standing in the ancient ways; although seventy per cent of them are bilingual, their outlook derives overwhelmingly from the Dutch and Calvinist peasant tradition of the Voortrekkers, and the refugee spirit that carried those hardy pioneers into the wilderness for sanctuary has not lost its hold upon them. It is very largely to the conservatism of the Free State that the Nationalist Party, playing upon the romantic associations that the word "Republic" still holds in Afrikaner minds, looks for electoral support.

There are very few urban concentrations in the Free State, and without a stop for more than a few minutes at a time the White Train went straight through from the Orange River to Bloemfontein, climbing all the way, for the city stands more than four thousand feet above the sea. At one small station, where the train stopped late at night, a fine prelude to the tour of the Province was furnished by a native choir, which sang the Hallelujah Chorus unaccompanied, the exultant chords of Handel's music ascending with superb effect in the summer dark.

March 7. Descending from the train in the morning to the accompaniment of a salute of twenty-one guns fired from Naval Hill, the Royal Family were immediately reminded that Bloemfontein is not only the seat of government for its own Province, but also the judicial capital of the Union itself. The first person to be presented to them by Dr. Colin Steyn, the Minister of Labour, who was now in attendance, was the Chief Justice of the Union, Mr. E. F. Watermeyer, who was accompanied by the other three Judges of the Court of Appeal. The procession was then formed with the additional state proper to the city's dignity, the royal cars being preceded by one of those escorts of mounted police which added so much to the grandeur of the greater ceremonies. Here may be an appropriate place to pay tribute to the splendid discipline and fine horsemanship of the South African Police Force, and to say that in both its mounted and dismounted branches its appearance on ceremonial occasions had no need to fear comparison with that of the military forces who habitually discharge in England many of the duties of attendance on the royal person which South African custom allots to the police. In addition to these processional appearances, the resources of the police force were taxed to the utmost by the laborious duties of traffic and crowd control incidental to the royal tour, while the separate force maintained by the railways had to provide a strong guard, which travelled from place to place to watch over the two trains wherever they halted. All the police were working prodigiously long hours; but their patience was never exhausted, and their blue uniforms and white helmets everywhere infused a sense of solidity and calm in the midst of

the excitement that seethed about the royal progress.

None of the state drives undertaken during the tour surpassed in dignity and spaciousness this procession through Bloemfontein; for with its broad avenues and well-proportioned buildings it has all the indefinable air of authority that belongs to a capital city. Decorations seemed to have a special elegance, which was still more noticeable after dark when the eye turned from the flags to the gracefully proportioned illuminations. The traditional republicanism of the people had caused some to harbour doubts what the reception might be. They need not have been anxious. The citizens of Bloemfontein have an urbane courtesy, and do not let their political principles interfere with their hospitality or their good manners. They made no noisy demonstration; few Afrikaners do. Among the flags the proportion of Tricolours to Union Jacks was naturally greater than in the Cape Province; but the orange, white and blue is quite properly regarded as the King's flag in his South African Dominion, and all along the route it was waving gallantly in his honour.

If the inherited simplicity of the Voortrekkers

Swaziland: homage of the Paramount Chief

Opening of the Gates of Memory, at the Cenotaph, Durban

guarantee that they cannot be affected by the baser kind of republican propaganda, of which it is scarcely necessary to say that the responsible members of the Nationalist party are never guilty. No one who made the acquaintance of the Royal Family in Bloemfontein is ever likely to listen again when he is told that these are foreigners, exercising an arbitrary authority from afar, and taking no personal interest in the South African people.

Owing to the dual character of the city, the state functions of the day were more elaborate than any that had been performed since leaving Cape Town. The *Radsaal*, which is the debating chamber of the Provincial Legislature, stands almost opposite to the City Hall, and the Royal Family were given a separate reception in each building. The Administrator, Dr. Barnard, welcomed the King with a formal oration at the *Radsaal* and then presented members of the legislature, with their wives; the King in his reply to the address accentuated the prevailing note of the day by sympathetic references to the "God-fearing ancestors" from whom the people of Bloemfontein derived their strength. The proceedings in the City Hall were less formal, since the address and reply were presented in writing; and after the town councillors and officials had made their bow on the platform, sovereign and subjects relaxed together in another of the pleasant morning tea parties of the country.

After tea the Royal Family drove to the small Government House of Bloemfontein, where they were to be lodged for the week-end, thus being able to sleep away from the train for the first time since they left Cape Town a fortnight before. They devoted the rest of the day to a series of social functions, beginning with a gathering of school children in the King's Park, where a choir of nearly a thousand boys and girls, in white shirts and blouses gleaming in the sun, sang hymns and

felt itself in any way out of tune with the royal magnificence, there was something else about the visitors which made perhaps more direct appeal here in Bloemfontein than anywhere else in the Union; and that was the equal simplicity of the Royal Family themselves, and especially of the Queen. One substantial burgher of Bloemfontein, commenting at the end of the first day on the immediate friendship that his fellow citizens felt had been established, remarked that after all his Trekker ancestors and the Presbyterian forbears of the Scottish Queen were fundamentally the same kind of people. That was probably the general feeling of Bloemfontein. It obviously has no direct political implications: it is not an argument either for or against the monarchy or republicanism. But its diffusion among the people does at least

Goedgegun: the Swazi dancers

songs of welcome; continuing with a crowded garden party in another part of the same park; and winding up the day with a civic ball. On the way back from the garden party they had driven round the streets of the native location, and alighted from their car for a few minutes to talk to some of the people who had gathered to cheer them.

Bloemfontein is one of the places where the gulf between the European and Bantu peoples, for which the Union of South Africa incurs so much criticism in the international sphere, is most conspicuous. About this time a report gained currency, and was even printed in a London newspaper, to the effect that the Union Government had given orders that no photographs illustrating the gracious demeanour always observed by the Royal Family towards the native and coloured peoples should appear in the press. This report may have been merely stupid, although it is difficult to believe that it was not malicious; it was certainly false. So far from attempting to impose a censorship of the kind suggested, the Government went out of its way to open up the subject to dispassionate observation. Every correspondent accredited to the royal tour was provided

Moolman, Swaziland

with a personal letter from Major Piet van der Byl, the Minister of Native Affairs, which authorized him, accompanied by a guide or alone as he might prefer, to enter any parts of the native reserves and locations, even those to which Europeans are not normally admitted, and to make any inquiries he might think fit. The policy of the Union towards the native races is intensely controversial, and is open to severe criticism; but its Ministers are guided by principles that they themselves conscientiously believe to be just, and by their conduct during the tour they made it very clear that they had no guilty secrets to conceal.

Having contrived to compress so full a programme into the first day of their visit to the capital of the Orange Free State, the Royal Family with the co-operation of their hosts were able to enjoy a week-end of relaxation. It included an informal visit to the home of Mrs. Steyn, widow of the last President of the republican Orange Free State—a gesture of personal sympathy and of respect for the Afrikaner tradition which was much appreciated in Bloemfontein.

March 8. On Saturday they left early in the morning by air for the Free State Game Reserve. The King's Flight was responsible for their transport, the King and Princess Margaret travelling in the first of the Vikings, and the Queen and Princess Elizabeth in the second. It was the first time that Princess Margaret had been in the air. They spent the day quietly, were given a *braaivleis* luncheon including some of those Afrikaner dishes of which the Queen especially was becoming fond, and were able to observe in their natural environment many varieties of buck and some of the birds of gorgeous plumage which abound in the forests of these sub-tropical latitudes. They were back at Government House in time to entertain the four Judges at dinner, together with their wives and Lady Duncan, the widow of the late Governor-General.

March 9. In the Cathedral next day the King was greatly touched to hear the Dean offer up a prayer specially composed for the occasion, in which on behalf of the people of South Africa he interceded for their fellow subjects in the United Kingdom, then passing through perhaps the cruellest phase of the bitter winter which had so terribly accentuated the privations following the war. Throughout the tour the one factor that marred the pleasure of the Royal Family in the glorious summer weather of Southern Africa and the splendid hospitality of its peoples was their anxiety over the sufferings of those whom they had left behind in the British Isles. This solemn and moving gesture, in the presence of God, by the Dean of Bloemfontein and the Free State congregation, exactly corresponded to the feeling that was in their hearts; and the King asked for a copy of the prayer, which he was to quote later on to another South African audience on an important occasion.

March 10. Next morning the Royal Family returned to the train and Mr. F. G. Bernadé, the Mayor, came down to the station to see them off. In his public career Mr. Bernadé has established

Goedgegun, Swaziland: The dance of Impenetrable Mystery

a consistent and honourable reputation as one of the ablest advocates of Nationalist principles. It is all the more due to him to record that during the royal stay in Bloemfontein he had done the honours of his city with the utmost courtliness, and set an example to the citizens of all races and political parties which undoubtedly was largely responsible for the cordial reception the King, the Queen and the Princesses had enjoyed. The thoughts of the people on the constitutional question may or may not show a modification in the coming years, when the long-term effects of the royal visit come to be estimated; but on the personal side the feelings of friendship between the Royal Family and their South African subjects had been as well established in Bloemfontein as in cities where acceptance of the monarchical idea is undisputed.

Kroonstad, the first town visited in the morning, seems destined to be a link between the past and present of the Free State, for it is only twenty miles—which in South Africa is a next-door-neighbour's distance—from Doornkloof, where Pretorius defeated the Zulu *impis* in the battle of Blood River on Dingaan's day in 1838, and it is close to the scene of the recent remarkable strike of gold. The question at the back of the mind of every man and woman in Kroonstad to-day is whether this little market town of seven thousand people is destined to expand, like Johannesburg half a century ago, into a vast and wealthy industrial city. But whether that is or is not to be the pattern of the Kroonstad of to-morrow, the Kroonstad of to-day is still one of the freshest and least sophisticated of South African communities. The royal reception took place in a pleasant park beside the river Vals, with a gentle breeze blowing among the willows and from time to time lifting the linen cloths which coyly and inadequately concealed the tea cups already laid out behind the

royal chairs. An amiable policeman posted within a few feet of the dais was taking photographs at high speed for members of the crowd, who passed him up their cameras and received them back at the rate of two or three to the minute. Everything was in fact as deliciously casual and intimate as it well could be.

Bethlehem, and the little river Jordan on which it stands, carry in their names evident reminders of the naïve piety of the Voortrekkers; and so do the inscriptions on the pathetic graves of Trekker children, which are dotted along the road by which the town is approached. The principal entertainment offered here to the Royal Family was a flower show, at which the Queen expressed the utmost admiration for the magnificence of the autumn blooms exhibited and was presented with some of the finest for the decoration of her rooms in the White Train. The other principal pride of Bethlehem was indicated as the royal party walked across the playing fields to the reception platform and read with a smile the notice: "No greater honour could befall the village cricketers of Bethlehem than that your gracious feet should cross their turf pitch." It should perhaps be observed for the benefit of English readers that in a land of matting wickets such a pitch is a rarity indeed.

March 11. With a short visit of an hour to Ladybrand the next morning, where there was another charming open-air concert by European and native choirs, the black children undoubtedly having the better of the comparison, the royal visit to the Orange Free State came to an end. It had been short; but the days spent among the vast spaces of the sunlit veld, and the hospitality of the little rural communities, had had a refreshing quality by which the royal travellers and all about them had been invigorated.

From Ladybrand the Royal Family travelled by road towards the approaches of the great Drakensberg range which is the principal watershed of South Africa and splits the country into two unequal parts of wholly different scenery and climate. The way runs across a majestic landscape in which cliffs and islands of rock seem to thrust themselves out of an ocean of undulant green. Here they crossed the little river Caledon and for a while left the Union of South Africa behind. The highland territory to which they had come is Basutoland, and its special place on the map of Africa is a monument to the genius of a great African. After the internecine wars of the terrible Chaka, a savage military despot who exercised as devastating an effect among the peoples of his own continent as his contemporary Napoleon Bonaparte did in Europe, a minor chief of the Bakoena, or "people of the crocodile," succeeded at last in rallying the broken remnants of many tribes in the natural fortresses provided by these rugged hills. His name was Moshesh, and for forty years he ruled over the peoples he had rescued, gradually welding them into a nation which now bears the name of Basuto. The great liberator was not always a benevolent governor or a good neighbour. For many years he was in conflict with the Voortrekker republic of the Orange Free State; and, even after he placed himself and his people under Queen Victoria's protection in 1868, it was more than once necessary for the British Government at the Cape to send military expeditions to call him to account. But his record stands as that of a great leader, who established law and order, albeit of a primitive kind, where previously had been starvation and chaos, and bequeathed to his people a robust tradition of loyalty to the British Crown under whose guardianship they have thriven. Basutoland belonged to none of the four colonies or republics that came to blows in 1899; it took no part in the South African war, and was not concerned with the Union of 1910. It is still administered as a Crown Colony under a High Commissioner, who is also the diplomatic representative accredited by the Government of the United Kingdom to that of the Union.

No one with any sensitiveness of mind can cross from the Union into Basutoland without feeling a remarkable change in the psychological atmosphere. The sense that the white and black races are in endless competition for the land and its amenities falls away at once. Basutoland is a black man's country, and the tiny white community is only there to help the natives make the best of it. The pride of the English administrators in the people they govern, and the confidence of the natives in their rulers, are everywhere self-evident. On the other hand, the contrast with the Union must not be laboured without full allowance for certain facts that tend the other way. There is a steady pressure of the Basuto upon the frontiers, always seeking the high industrial wages obtainable within the Union, which many of them undoubtedly consider to be more than a compensation for any social inferiority that the Union system inflicts on the Bantu. In other words, Basutoland, and for that matter Swaziland and Bechuanaland, which are controlled in a similar way by the same High Commissioner, fundamentally resemble the native reservations within the Union itself. They are relics of an older Africa, where something like the

Lovedale: singing before the King

Chief Tshekedi and Chief Bathoene

primitive tribal life can still be lived as it was before the coming of the white man; but it is lived at the cost of a continuance of the poverty which has beset black Africa from time immemorial. The black man everywhere has been tempted by the superior material resources of the white to claim admission into the Europeanized social order; and the time when this irresistible

stripes were lined up at the prison fence and shouted cheerfully with the rest.

The Basuto are above all things a nation of horsemen. For many days before the arrival of the royal party at Maseru, the frontier post where the great national assembly or "Pitso" was to be held, they had been riding in from every part of their mountain country. Some of them had come hun-

The Oudstryders.

urge brings about the transformation of the High Commission Territories is no doubt only postponed.

Meanwhile, however, the great tradition of paternal imperialism prevails in Basutoland; and as the royal procession drove between miles of grinning black faces, it was impossible to listen to the booming cheers of the men and the shrill ululations of the women who, contrary to local convention, had in many places found a place among them, without the sense that this was a happy people. Even the convicts in red and white

dreds of miles. There were estimated to be sixty or seventy thousand of them present, mostly clothed in the many-coloured blankets with which the Basuto muffle themselves even on days—as was this one—when the temperature runs up to the region of a hundred in the shade. Not that there was any shade to speak of at Maseru. Immediately on crossing the frontier Their Majesties were received by the High Commissioner, Sir Evelyn Baring, and the King inspected a parade of white ex-service men and a black guard of honour comprising both infantry and cavalry contingents.

Pretoria : the Transvaal Museum

Then began the drive along the ranks of mounted men who lined one side of the road for miles and, after the royal cars had passed, fell into a cantering column behind. The great cloud of dust which their horses' hooves threw up seemed to incommode them little; and the impromptu and jubilant cavalcade which escorted the King of Basutoland like a conqueror home will long be a thrilling memory to those who watched it.

The day came to a romantically beautiful end with a great display of fireworks, probably the first that most of the Basuto had ever seen. The Royal Family sat in chairs on the grass of the Pitso ground, so close to the operators that one falling star was caught by the Queen's secretary in his hat, and a rocket burned a small hole in Princess Elizabeth's dress. Again and again the rising and falling lights lit up the figure of the Queen and were reflected from her tiara; and every time this happened great waves of cheers went rolling round the crowded acres, where it was

thought that over a hundred thousand people were gathered.

March 12. There could have been no fewer the next morning, when the Pitso proper was held. Daylight revealed the ground as an immense natural amphitheatre, which was densely packed with vast multitudes of men, those on foot drawn up in front while the thousands of horsemen sat their ponies in ranks behind. A few Chiefs in front wore impressive karosses of leopard skin; at their head was Mantsebo Seeiso, appearing as regent for her nephew the Paramount Chief, who is a boy of twelve now being educated at a mission school. A riderless foal, which had somehow insinuated itself among the cavaliers, having been pursued for about two hundred yards down the processional route by a stately mounted officer with drawn sword, and hustled out of sight just in time, the two royal cars drove up to the platform accompanied by a Sovereign's escort of cavalry, the first to be mounted anywhere in the Empire since the outbreak of war in 1939.

The applause that greeted the royal appearance was like a tidal wave of sound, seeming to flow down from the very mountains themselves. The High Commissioner in his speech of welcome referred to the notable services of the Basuto in the Pioneer Corps, whose badge was cut out of the grass of a hillside overlooking the Pitso ground, in very much the same way as the immemorial White Horses of southern England. In reply, the King made a moving acknowledgment of the debt he owed to this small people, who had aided him "at a time when I was beset with many and powerful enemies." The Regent Chief also spoke, and dwelt significantly on her people's desire to retain their present position under the Colonial Office and the Crown.

The King then proceeded to invest Basuto soldiers and civilians with decorations they had won during the war, and there were several very touching scenes as men and women were reduced almost to tears of joy by the honour of shaking the hand of the Sovereign who had for so long been the unseen object of their patriotic devotion. The leading Chiefs, as at all similar indabas inside and outside the Union, were given silver medallions struck at the Mint in London to commemorate the royal tour. In the afternoon the European community were entertained to a garden party, during which the King held a second investiture; Princess Elizabeth and Princess Margaret reviewed the Basuto Girl Guides. They took special interest in a closed omnibus which appeared on the parade and on inquiry proved to contain twenty Guides who were suffering from leprosy. The two Princesses insisted on going over and talking to these unfortunates.

March 13. Leaving Basutoland on the morning of Thursday, March 13, the White Train passed again over a corner of Free State territory and stopped for an hour at Harrismith. The Royal

Pretoria : one of the University buildings

Family made the usual tour of the streets, and outside the town hall, where they were entertained to a morning tea party, saw one of the most striking symbols of reconciliation in the Province. Opposite to one another stood, on the one side a memorial to the men of the Second Battalion Grenadier Guards and Second Battalion Scots Guards who fell in the South African War, and on the other an archway erected in honour of the Boers who died fighting against them. Princess Elizabeth, as Colonel of the Grenadiers, had a photograph taken of the Guards memorial, with the intention of sending it to the editor of the regimental magazine.

Pretoria: Union Buildings and Botha's statue

THE PROVINCE OF NATAL

IN the afternoon the Royal Family said good-bye at Marseilles to Dr. Barnard, the Administrator of the Orange Free State, and were received on the platform at Ladysmith by the Administrator of Natal, Mr. D. E. Mitchell, and Mrs. Mitchell. Natal is a province of two-fold origin, the Voortrekkers having reached its western parts by land in the course of their perilous journey over the Drakensberg at almost the same time as the English began to penetrate from the sea and were developing the harbour of Port Natal or Durban. Its name is very much older, having been conferred by Vasco da Gama in com-memoration of the fact that he first sighted its shores on Christmas Day, 1497 (*Natalis* is the Latin for birthday).

The immense commercial importance of Durban has long since given to the English element a pre-dominance over the Afrikaner that it enjoys no-where else in the Union; and politically, therefore, Natal is the mainstay of orthodox royalist and imperial principles. Outside parliamentary politics, however, there is another very important element to be considered. It was to Natal, the province of the sugar plantations, that the first Indian immigrants were introduced nearly a hundred years ago; and

Indian dancers at Pietermaritzburg

Port Elizabeth: ceremony of signing the Golden Book

Pretoria City Hall

to-day the Indian community, though not enjoying the parliamentary vote, is nearly as numerous as the two European races put together. Legislation in Natal, particularly that relating to the acquisition of land, has long been directed to checking the growth of Indian influence. There is an ever-present fear lest the immigrants, with their high birth-rate and low standard of living, may eventually transform Natal from a European into an Asiatic province. The disabilities thus imposed upon Indians have involved the Union in a quarrel with India itself; Indian propaganda against South Africa has been active in the international sphere, and largely as a consequence the United Nations, only a few weeks before the beginning of the royal tour, formally censured the policy of the Union towards its Indian subjects. (The reply of General Smuts's Government, to the effect that the people alleged to be oppressed were nearly all born in South Africa, and are therefore Union

and not Indian nationals, with its corollary that the question is domestic and not international and so lies outside the sphere of the United Nations, seems unanswerable in law.) The dispute was still rumbling on when the royal party reached the frontiers of Natal, and the Natal Indian Congress had called upon its members to boycott all the royal ceremonies. Accordingly there was bound to be anxiety lest Natal should prove an exception to the rule of harmony which had hitherto been unbroken.

Ladysmith, the first big town to be visited, takes its name from the beautiful Spanish bride whom the future Sir Harry Smith had brought home with him from his active service as a subaltern in the Peninsular War. It is a place full of history, most famous perhaps for the long and arduous siege that the British garrison sustained there in 1899 and 1900. It was no doubt not a coincidence that the Prime Minister had himself chosen to assume the functions of Minister in Attendance on the King just before the Royal Family came to Ladysmith; and as he walked with the royal party round the recreation ground of the Oval, where the presentations were made and King, Queen and Princesses signed the Distinguished Visitors' Book, his strategic eye ranged keenly over the historic ground he had such good reason to know well. The King listened with profound interest as the distinguished veteran pointed out the tactical features of the surrounding hills, whence his own batteries had once commanded the fortress he never quite reduced. To have seen the great soldier-statesman drive into the undefeated city as the chief servant and friend in South Africa of the Sovereign of the victorious Empire is to have witnessed one of the symbolic events of history, and to have stood for a moment under the spell of high chivalry. In that spirit it seemed to be taken by the old soldiers on the parade of ex-service men, who crowded round the Prime Minister and cheered him again and again; and this great personal reception, so far from

diminishing, seemed to enhance the warmth of the welcome given to the Royal Family. That welcome extended itself along streets lined by native men and women to the Wagon Bridge ground, where the main native gathering, headed by the local Chiefs, was assembled, and where Their Majesties for the first time met contingents bearing the ceremonial shields, monkey-tail costumes, and feathered head-dresses of the Zulu race. Moreover, a good omen was observed even on this first stop in Natal. The Indians were taking their full share in the reception. Groups of Indian women in many-coloured *saris* were as conspicuous in the streets as they were picturesque, and the men were quite as numerous. Ladysmith is not one of the great centres of Indian population. But it was at least encouraging to note that, as a well-informed local resident estimated, at least half the Indians of the town were in the streets, mostly wearing loyal favours, and cheering for the King Emperor. The authorities of the Natal Indian Congress would certainly stick to their guns; but it looked already as if their constituents were

Kruger National Park: watching the hippopotami

lukewarm in support of their uncompromising attitude.

Now came a holiday and an interlude. The King, Queen and Princesses left Ladysmith by road in the afternoon to spend a long week-end in the seclusion of the Natal National Park. Although not the richest in wild life, this great area of mountain and forest is the most beautiful of the national parks which are the special glory of South Africa. The Royal Family were

ness fell, an electric storm flashed and blinked among the peaks, revealing for an instant, almost as if they actually overhung the buildings, precipices and chasms and the serrated outline of the *massif*. Here was nature at its wildest and mightiest.

March 14-17. In these surroundings the Royal Family enjoyed four days of seclusion, with the simple pleasures of the country, walking, climbing, bathing, and fishing. The Field-Marshal was still with them and was able to tell them much more

Pretoria: the civic welcome

lodged at the Natal Government Hostel, which sits in the lap of the Drakensberg mountains, four thousand eight hundred feet above the sea. The mountains, dominated by the towering peaks of Mont Aux Sources, eleven thousand one hundred and fifty feet high, and the Sentinel, only four hundred feet lower, enclose a mighty amphitheatre; and against their sombre background the terraced gardens of the hostel blazed with the colour of their autumn flowers. On the first evening there was a great massing of dark thunder clouds beyond the ranges, and as the light faded they seemed oppressive and sinister. When dark-

about the campaigns of his youth, guiding them afterwards over parts of the battlefields of Spion Kop and Colenso, which lie close to the boundaries of the National Park. He told them of such famous episodes as the gallant exploit of Lieutenant Roberts, son of the Commander-in-Chief, in his effort to save the guns at Colenso, when he won the V.C. and received his mortal wound; and of the capture of Winston Churchill by General Botha in person at the ambush of the armoured train at Frere. It was at this station, which preserves the name of Sir Bartle Frere, an eminent mid-Victorian Governor of the Cape, that the

Bloemfontein Aerodrome

royal party rejoined the White Train on the afternoon of March 17.

March 18. If the Transkei was a land of song, Natal, as represented by its capital, Pietermaritzburg (named after the celebrated Voortrekker leader Pieter Maritz), impressed itself on the memory as a country of the dance. The Royal Family went through the usual routine of a state entry into a new province, being received with a salute of guns as the train drew into the station and going on to the city hall to listen to addresses of welcome from the Administrator of the Province and the Mayor of the city. Mrs. Russell was the first lady holding such an office whom they had yet met, and she spoke her few words of greeting with great dignity. There followed the customary drive through streets lined with cheering crowds. But it is the dances that remain in the memory. The first was performed by schoolgirls on the cricket ground. Some dressed in the colours of the United King-

Princess Elizabeth at Government House, Salisbury, with the Deputation of 5 children, representing the white and coloured school children who contributed to the Gift

dom and some in those of the Union, they tripped in light and merry measures, matching the cool sunlight of a perfect autumn day. It was a lovely and gracious sight; but honesty must acknowledge that it was eclipsed in the afternoon when Their Majesties were entertained by the Indian community. Here was increasing evidence that the boycott was not to be allowed to impair the courtesy of the Indian reception of the Royal Family, whether that courtesy could or could not be legitimately interpreted as extending to political loyalty. Certainly the Indians of Pietermaritzburg turned out in their thousands to cheer resoundingly. The loveliest display of the day was given by fifty

Indian girls, who exhibited "the charm of woven paces and of waving hands" with the liquid grace that only the *sari* can preserve. In triangle and in circle they moved with a hieratic stateliness that might have come down out of the past of immemorial India and yet clearly held the spirit of a living civilization. Line and colour and sound (for the dance was accompanied on Indian tambourines) seemed to project ancient Asia into timeless Africa; but in the presence of the Sovereign who unites them there was no incongruity. At the end of the dance the Indians, hundreds of whom had been waving Union Jacks all the time, sang "God Save the King" with enthusiasm; then with equal fervour they sang "Die Stem van Suid Africa," and that, in the existing state of relations between India and the Union, was greater evidence of the healing power of the royal visit. A civic garden party rounded off Pietermaritzburg's welcome to its royal guests.

March 19. Postponing their formal visit to Durban, the suburbs of which the White Train merely skirted during the night, the Royal Family arrived early next morning at Gingindhlovu, and went on by road from this small border post to Eshowe, which in colonial days was the administrative capital of Zululand. In contrast to their formidable military reputation, the Zulus inhabit a land of gentler scenery than the tour had lately traversed; it is a country of red soil very like that of Devon, and even the omnipresent sugar plantations did not take away from a general impression of rolling downland which might have been part of Exmoor. In the speech of welcome offered to Their Majesties by

Albert Luthuli, the representative Chief, in which deep veneration was expressed for the memory of Queen Victoria, who had received the Zulu nation into her clemency and favour after eventually defeating them in the terrible Zulu Wars, the picturesque imagery of the race was vividly employed. King George, for instance, was compared to the elephant whose tread shakes the earth, and to the lion whose roaring causes all the rest of creation to be respectfully silent.

After presentation of medallions to Chief Cyprian, heir of the Zulu Royal Family, and other leading Chiefs, a wide space in front of the platform was cleared for a performance of the ancient Zulu royal dances. This was in the nature of an experiment, for nothing on a great scale had been attempted in this kind for many years, and the exhibition would involve the revival of ceremonies belonging to a social order which is already nearly obsolete. There is no place in modern Africa for the ferocious *impis* of Chaka and Dingaan; and with their absorption within the framework of a more sophisticated society the tribal system of which they were the military expression has been largely superseded. The Zulus of to-day are a peaceful agricultural community; and a large proportion of the grandsons of the terrible warriors of Isandhlwana are now in quiet municipal employment in Durban. If it has to be said that the war dances displayed before the King had an air of artificiality about them, that is really not surprising. These people were, in fact, playing in a historical pageant; they were playing, no doubt, with a real pride in their own stirring past, but the suggestion of amateur theatricals which clings to all pageants could not altogether be kept out.

The weaker side of the spectacle was mostly to be seen in its early stages. The first great column of warriors, who went wheeling round the arena, clad in ox-hides and vulture feathers and carrying the shields and assegais of the ancient *impis*, seemed a little shy of their own imposing panoply, and though they crouched and sprang with athletic energy, did so a little shamefacedly like schoolboys in fancy dress. But those in the audience who knew the country well advised the visitors to wait; the Zulus, they said, are notoriously slow to warm up. They are slowest of all when, as had happened on this occasion, the supply of kaffir beer had

been prudently cut short for a day or two before the visit of an important person. Unnaturally abstemious as this dusky *corps de ballet* had been rendered for the occasion, there might, said the experts, be something more exciting to come.

So it proved. It was the women who did away with the air of self-consciousness. The long lines of Zulu girls, their bare skins glistening like polished leather above their short kilts, who danced in slow rhythm up to the royal platform, showed from their first emergence into the arena a more cheerful and spontaneous spirit; and, when their first rush was exhausted, they stood in panting lines, grinning and giggling and evidently as reluctant as some leading actresses of fairer complexion to surrender the centre of the stage. So the regiment of warriors who were to charge in the next scene had practically to hunt them off. In the process the men in turn seemed to shed their former diffidence, and with tossing plumes and brandished knobkerries infused a new sense of passion into their concerted movement.

This was the end of self-consciousness. A great wave of spearmen swept up to the very steps of the royal stand, almost shaking the earth with the stamp of naked feet; and, as it recoiled and eddied away, individual warriors came prancing forth from the ranks and competed with one another in ever more fantastic caperings. These solo turns, which were going on all over the arena at the same time, were scarcely suspended even when the beaded girls swung out into the middle for another massed movement ; and meanwhile one middle-aged lady in leopard skins, taking apparently no notice of the programme or any other performer, caracoled round and about, whinnying like a horse. The royal salute *Bayete*, which in the early stages had been pronounced almost apologetically, was now declaimed with a more sonorous power, and varied with other chants of simple homage to the King. After taking some time to work up, the Zulu people were evidently feeling their way back into the spirit of their ancestors. They did not quite recapture the dark passion of the days of Chaka; but certainly they had got a long way beyond the artificiality of Hollywood. Perhaps to say that their exhibition was at least first-class Rider Haggard is neither to flatter nor unjustly to depreciate.

March 20. After this long detour to the north-west the White Train returned in the morning of March 20 and came down for the first time to the shores of the Indian Ocean. The city of Durban, although its harbour was sighted from the sea by Vasco da Gama, really takes its origin from a small missionary station planted there by a retired officer of the Royal Navy, Captain Allen Gardiner, in 1835. On that occasion the name of Port Natal, which had been borne for centuries by a harbour whose vast potentialities had not yet been recognized, was changed to Durban in honour of Sir Benjamin D'Urban, then Governor of the Cape. Its history for the next twenty years is largely concerned with the struggle for control between the English settlers and the Voortrekkers coming down from the Drakensberg; and it was in this conflict that the ancestral hero of Durban, Dick King, achieved his fame. The little garrison of two hundred and fifty men, who were defending the town in 1842, were defeated in a skirmish at Congella, and besieged in what is now the Old Fort. Dick King escaped from the Fort, swam the bay, took horse the other side, and in ten days rode the six hundred miles over the mountains to Grahamstown, then the most easterly outpost of the Cape. The reinforcements he summoned raised the siege of the Old Fort; and Dick King's statue stands on the esplanade to-day to commemorate his exploit. The successful defence, which he made possible, settled the issue between

Chief Imwiko's state barge on the Zambesi

English and Dutch; Natal became a dependency of the Cape instead of the Free State, and in 1856 became a Crown Colony in its own right.

Durban to-day is a city of many races, and such characteristic sights as that of rickshaws bowling along the streets behind Zulu boys clothed in leopard skins and with tall erections of feathers on their heads give it an atmosphere which is in some ways exotic even by the standards of South Africa. Nevertheless architecturally its predominantly English inhabitants have given it very much the appearance of a big English seaside town. When the Royal Family arrived its broad avenues and esplanades were filled with an excited crowd, all cheering in a curiously English manner. There seemed to be a general determination to make the royal visitors feel particularly at home by surrounding them with an atmosphere as closely as possible resembling that which they had left behind on the shores of the Channel. The other races of the city were of course present in full strength; but neither Dutch nor Zulus nor Indians —and there were plenty of these to be seen— express their loyalty with quite the continuous uproar of the English when they give their minds to it.

Outside the City Hall, where the formal reception and presentation of notabilities took place, a great square was crowded to its utmost capacity with people; the roofs and balconies were

also thronged, and young enthusiasts were climbing perilously up the lamp-posts to get a better view. It was all very suggestive of Piccadilly Circus on a day of national rejoicing. Everybody seemed to have a Union Jack to wave; only here and there the Tricolour reminded the exultant English that there was another race with equal rights and its own way of expressing its loyalty. This was in fact by far the most demonstrative welcome the Royal Family received anywhere in South Africa. But in recording, as is just, that Durban, which had obviously set out to surpass all its rivals in sheer volume of cheering, succeeded in its object, it would be quite unfair to imply that other cities which were less vocal were therefore less hospitable or less patriotic. The Afrikaners are by comparison with the English a dour and silent folk; and the King and Queen very soon learned to appreciate that the mute admiration and wonder with which they were greeted in some of the mainly Afrikaans-speaking towns were there the highest compliment they could be paid.

After the usual morning tea party the Royal Family came out again from the City Hall and drove round the square to open the Gate of Remembrance, which had been added to the city's cenotaph to commemorate the men of Natal who had fallen in the second world war. For a moment the tumultuous cheering of the crowd was hushed, and a deeper emotion than exultation took its place, as the august melancholy of "Last Post," sounded by the bugles of the Royal Durban Light Infantry, spoke to the multitudes of sacrifice and pride and bereavement and of a light shining beyond the darkness. Then the King turned the key of the gate, opened one leaf of its double doors, and passed through. The Queen walked at his side; but noticing that the other leaf of the doors was still closed, she turned back and gently and solemnly swung it open herself. The little episode, not only associating the Queen in the ceremony, but perhaps by implication suggesting the part of the women of the Empire side by side with their men in a victory achieved in unprecedented manner by the common effort of the whole people, seemed to catch the imagination of the crowd, and was greeted with subdued cheering that lasted for a long time.

That evening the royal party returned to the City Hall, where the Mayor and Mayoress were giving a ball in their honour. It was possibly the hottest night they were to know during the whole of their tour of the Union; and the humidity of the atmosphere, for which Durban is notorious, caused some of the most enthusiastic and athletic of the dancers to wilt. But nothing seemed to check the ardour of the two Princesses, who danced energetically through most of the evening, and contrived to look not only radiant but comparatively cool to the end. As at last the royal party left at midnight for King's House, where they were to spend the week-end, the Mayor and Mayoress, who said good-bye to them at the top of the steps, watched the cars out of sight, and then fell into one another's arms and embraced. The pleasant little incident vividly conveyed to many minds the anxieties that must have beset innumerable officials responsible for the entertainment of the exalted visitors up and down a country whose experience of high ceremonial is naturally limited, and the relief that must come to them when a great event has been successfully surmounted and all has gone according to plan.

March 21. On Friday, Durban held its children's day, and thirty thousand boys and girls assembled in the stands of the racecourse to see the King and Queen. This was in a plain and calculated sense Durban's reply to Port Elizabeth; everybody in the town had read the accounts in the newspapers, and was determined to go one better than the rival port. By the test of numbers of course they succeeded, for Durban is much the larger town; as to quality, an English writer must not presume to draw comparisons. The argument is believed to be still in progress between the champions of the two communities. Port Elizabeth had concentrated upon song. Durban went in for drama. As soon as the royal party had taken their places on the platform, facing the grandstands, the green course between them began to flood with a tide of boys and girls. The boys were symbolically dressed in jerseys of blue, purple, or green of several shades intended to represent the sea, the mountains, the rivers, and the veld which have made the character of South Africa; the girls were in petalled frocks of many colours to portray the rich variety of the country's flowers, from the garden lily to the majestic protea. All races were represented in the pageant, and it was particularly pleasing to listen to the applause of the European

Salisbury—opening Parliament in the House of Assembly

children as the native contingents moved into their places in the great design. When all were in position in the final tableau the whole multitude of children, the five thousand on the course and the twenty-five thousand in the stands, broke into the strains of "Land of Hope and Glory." As its last notes faded they all produced concealed flags and waved them with wild enthusiasm for many minutes on end. This was perhaps the supreme moment of visible and audible patriotism in the whole tour.

March 22. This second day in Durban having ended with a garden party in Mitchell Park, the morrow was devoted to making contact with the adult citizens of Durban in the mass. On the aerodrome the King and Queen appeared in the presence of an immense crowd of natives, estimated to number no less than a hundred thousand.

Durban, the largest in the Union, had assembled to cheer them. Here, beyond dispute, the Congress boycott finally collapsed. Captain Boycott himself would have had little to complain of if left with only sixty-five thousand people to keep him company.

In West Street, near the City Hall, the M.O.T.H.'s—which initials denote the Memorable Order of Tin Hats—marched past the King. Over twenty-three thousand ex-service men and women were on parade; and the remarkable physical fitness and soldierly bearing of the older men particularly impressed Their Majesties. A number of artificial legs went past at the same rapid pace as the younger and uninjured contingents. A high officer of Scotland Yard, who had seen many military displays, remarked that it was probably the smartest parade of its kind that the

Johannesburg: Mascot of the Imperial Light Horse

The arrangements were not altogether perfect, for it was obvious that the authorities had quite failed to foresee how vast would be the concourse, and the failure to provide sufficient food and water or transport home added a good deal to the discomforts of the long wait in the overpowering heat. Nevertheless, it was the pure impulse of loyalty that had brought all these tens of thousands of people together; and, making light of the rather numerous faints and other casualties, they expressed that loyalty with touching fervour. The royal party went on to Currie's Fountain, where it seemed that the whole Indian community of

King and Queen had seen since the war. It was not only the marchers who were required to show their physical endurance; in the torrid heat the King himself remained at the salute, and the Queen and Princesses standing, for forty minutes without a rest.

In the afternoon the royal party spent a little time at the races, fortunately leaving before the occurrence of an unhappy scene, when a disagreement between the judges and the bulk of the spectators as to which of several horses had come in first in a neck-and-neck finish led to something like a riot, and the premature abandonment of the meeting.

Salisbury: His Majesty's escort of Mounted Police

Dancers and drummers on the banks of the Zambesi

March 24. The last town to be visited in Natal was Vryheid. The name, which is the Afrikaans for freedom, enshrines the curious origin of the place. In the year 1884 two rival chiefs, Dinizulu and Sibepu, were at war for the supremacy of the Zulu nation; and Dinizulu enlisted the services of a number of farmers from the Transvaal and the Free State to fight for him on a promise of a reward in land. With their aid he defeated his rival, and in fulfilment of his promise ceded three million acres to them. On this territory the Afrikaners built the town of Vryheid and proclaimed what they called the New Republic, with their leader, Lucas Meyer, as its first president. But its so-called freedom was mainly dependent on the authority of Dinizulu; and when that potentate was deposed in 1888 the New Republic came to a speedy end. Its territory was first annexed by the Transvaal, and in 1900 transferred to Natal. It is now a very peaceful little community, with a double source of prosperity in its agriculture and its coal mines, and the Royal Family are likely to remember it best for the particularly pleasant morning tea party they enjoyed in a tent erected some distance out in the bushveld, under the brow of a hill and with a charming outlook over a placid lake below.

The Royal launch on the Zambesi

TRANSVAAL PROVINCE AND SWAZILAND

MARCH 24–25. The White Train crossed the frontier of the Transvaal in the afternoon of Monday, March 24; but the next morning the royal party left it for a flying visit by road to Swaziland. This little country of less than seven thousand square miles is the second of the High Commission Territories which preserve the colonial form of government in the midst of the provinces of the Union of South Africa. Once more the High Commissioner and Lady Mary Baring were waiting at the frontier to receive the royal party; but they were inconspicuous figures in comparison with the four gorgeously bedecked Swazi warriors who mounted guard at the point

Queenstown: a bouquet for the Princess too

H.R.H. Princess Elizabeth

Presenting Colours at Pretoria

of reception, and with the two high dignitaries of the country who were waiting to make their obeisance.

One of these was the Paramount Chief Sobhuza Dlamini II, who had obtained for the occasion, from some sartorial artist who deserves a wider fame, a uniform in the height of the military fashion of the Second Empire. It included a tunic of armorial azure, trousers of blazing scarlet, gold epaulettes, and a lemon-coloured sash crossing diagonally from the shoulder to the waist. In contrast with this polychromatic figure the Queen Mother, who stood beside him, was bare-footed and clothed in a costume entirely of skins, which it was easy to believe had not been changed for many years. The lady, who bears the title of "the she elephant," exercises magical powers over the rainfall, and if she changed her clothes the effects on the crops would be disastrous. There was, in fact, a light rain falling while the party waited for the arrival of the royal procession; but the Queen Mother blandly explained that she had herself arranged for this, in order to lay the dust during His Majesty's long journey from Moolman across the Transvaal frontier. The weather, she said, would clear in time for the ceremonies of the day; and so it did. Bizarre as both the two native dignitaries appeared to European eyes, when they took their places in the indaba at Goedgegun they performed their allotted parts with a measured dignity that was truly impressive.

The proceedings at the indaba showed the double aspect of the life of the Swazis, who within their own boundaries preserve much of their tribal system and ancestral traditions, and yet have made their mark in another continent. The latter aspect was typified in the march past of the Swazi Pioneer Corps, who strode along in British khaki uniform at a swinging pace that seemed to declare their pride in the battle honours they had won so far away as the beaches of Anzio. But they were succeeded in the arena by a phalanx of warriors of an older fashion, perhaps a thousand in number, who surged forward towards the royal platform in the slow rhythm of the "dance of impenetrable mystery," which is the ancient salute accorded to visitors of the highest degree.

No women take part in these great spectacles. The men, all in leopard-skin girdles, with gleaming black skins, and their towering head-dresses looking like a thicket of feathers, carried their assegais and knobkerries with a suggestion of menace that gave a very real idea of how formidable must have been the *impis* of the ancient wars. They swung their big ox-hide shields out and down in homage, and they hailed the King with an eerie whistle between clenched teeth, which is the Swazi form of the royal salute. There was no suggestion of fancy dress in their display; it was impossible to doubt that this stately dance came out of the living customs of the country. When the royal party reluctantly left to keep their luncheon engagement at the Residency and to attend the official garden party afterwards, the dance was still going on, and in fact the warriors kept it up far into the afternoon.

March 26. With General Pienaar, Administrator of the Transvaal, now acting as principal guide to his province, the royal party next day took to the road and travelled over nearly a hundred miles of the high veld to visit two of its smaller towns. The first of these, Ermelo, contrived to give an individual quality to its welcome by parading a commando of farmers at the municipal boundary to escort the royal party to the town hall. This old word "commando," which has had so honourable a revival in the second world war, was once a name of ill omen to British troops. In South African usage it stands for the ancient unit of light irregular horse, raised by compulsory levy all over the agricultural regions of the Boer republics. Every man was trained to act without orders on his own initiative, and the whole body could disappear into practical invisibility even in the most naked regions of the veld. It was these commandos of the old regime that transformed the tactics of modern war by teaching their enemies through bitter experience the paramount necessity of open-order formation and the utmost possible use of cover. The commandos of to-day are all volunteer units; and the practical disappearance of cavalry from the battlefield makes it improbable that they will ever fight again after the old manner. But the old organization is kept up, and the old horsemanship and the old consummate veldcraft have not been allowed to decline. The hundred men of the commando who met the King at Ermelo included some who were young enough to wear the medal ribbons of the recent war; but many wore with equal pride the green and orange ribbon that commemorated service under Botha or Smuts, Cronje or De Wet, in the campaigns of long ago.

Young and old seemed now equally proud to be escorting the Sovereign of the Union into their town, and the eldest of them all, aged over seventy, stammered out his expression of loyalty with eyes moist with emotion. It was a romantic link with the stormy past when this cavalcade, riding jauntily yet with simple dignity, fell into column of threes in front of the royal car, and led their King and Queen to meet the people of Ermelo.

After appearing in the customary manner, first before the Europeans and then before the natives of Ermelo, the procession drove off at a high speed to cross sixty miles of open veld, sprinkled beautifully with mauve and white wild flowers, to Standerton, where the party assembled to welcome them at the Magistrates' Court was headed by the Prime Minister, who represents the town in the House of Assembly. Nothing more charming was seen in the whole tour than the entertainment to which General Smuts invited the Royal Family after the formal business of speeches and presentations had been completed. On the show grounds outside the town an *al fresco* luncheon was served by the ladies of Standerton, and while the Royal Family sat at table a display of folk dancing was given.

Folk dancing is a name that has covered a multitude of sins. Sometimes it stands for the false antique, in the most pretentious and artificial style. But the folk dancing of Standerton was manifestly the real thing. There were twelve couples, the men in white flannels and the women in long dresses and bonnets of pastel colours. They stepped gaily and swiftly through a succession of country dances, singing softly, as they circled, the gentle and happy Afrikaans folk songs, and accompanied by a *Boers Orches* of accordions and fiddles. Apart from the lovely rhythms of the dance, what caught the eye most of all was the expression of pride and joy on the face of every one of the dancers; it might have been interpreted as affection for one another, or equally as delight in the presence of their King and Queen a few yards away. But in either case it gave the idea that Standerton was pre-eminently a "city that is at unity in itself"—a unity that, if it existed before

the King came, was nevertheless completed and exalted by his presence. The Royal Family had been, as it were, taken into the heart of a peasant tradition that perhaps reached back even beyond the Voortrekkers into the life of the European Netherlands. Artistically this was the most exquisite moment of the tour.

March 27. The following day the Royal Family withdrew themselves from their human subjects in order to seek out some of the infinite variety of four-footed creatures who inhabit their South African dominions. The Kruger National Park is not the least of the memorials to qualities of the last President of the Transvaal which are sometimes underestimated in England, where he is commonly regarded as a narrow-minded man. But it is to his government that belongs the credit for the great and imaginative act of setting aside in 1896 an area of no less than eight thousand square miles, which is as large as Wales, to be preserved for ever as a sanctuary for the native wild animals of the country. Every kind of animal, from the elephant and the lion downwards, there ranges free; the hunter is excluded, but for the unarmed lover of wild life the park is for most of the year freely open as a holiday resort. The animals seem to have learned that within these confines man may be treated as a friend, and they venture with little sign of fear up to the very edges of the motor roads, and even stand to watch the cars go past at a distance of only a few yards.

Perhaps a mistake was made in allowing quite so many cars to follow the Royal Family round the park; but the King was in a holiday mood, and apparently wished to interfere with nobody's enjoyment. He himself drove the Queen for most of the day, and the Princesses followed in a separate car.

No lion disputed the sovereignty of the bushveld with the human monarch, although some members of the household caught a glimpse of two distant lionesses. Their claim did not go undisputed, but was eventually put beyond a doubt by the testimony of a press photographer, who had brought with him a telephoto lens. Elephants showed their recent presence only by their spoor. But the royal party saw great herds of dainty impala grazing by the roadside or leaping through the bush, together with many zebra, a few giraffe, and sometimes a stately koodoo bull looking disdainfully down

from the top of some mighty boulder. The burly blue wildebeeste was also conspicuous, and the Princesses jubilantly scored a point by detecting a couple of wart hogs which their parents had missed. Although the cortège at some points extended almost to forty cars, most of these animals stood quite unperturbed to watch the procession go by. Even so timid a beast as a jackal, whose presence the local experts took as evidence that a lion had made a recent kill in the vicinity, stayed at gaze for several minutes before slipping away into the undergrowth. Birds of brilliant plumage, apes and baboons looked down from the tree-tops.

In the afternoon the royal party visited a reach of the Sabi River which is frequented by hippopotami, and saw as many as six of these great creatures simultaneously thrusting their noses out of the water and blowing up clouds of spray. The King and Queen watched this spectacle for half an hour before finishing their tour of the park at the rest camp of Pretoriuskop, a little village of white-washed round huts rather like a glorified Kaffir kraal, which the Government maintains for the benefit of holiday makers.

March 28. Since there lay immediately ahead another great programme of State functions, the next day had been left practically free of official engagements. But, as occasionally happened on the tour, an unofficial contribution to the entertainment of the Royal Family proved one of the most delightful. The White Train had to wait for some hours at the small station or siding of Westaffin. It happens to adjoin one of the biggest fruit farms of the Transvaal, to which the growers of tomatoes and mangoes, adopting Lewis Carroll's rules for the formation of portmanteau words, have given the happy name of Tomango. The two thousand labourers of the Tomango farm, who are mostly Swazis, had been given a day's holiday and had assembled in a hollow semi-circle facing the line where the White Train would draw up. In the open space paraded a team of about fifty dancers, including a few women, all flaunting the most vivid colours possible, with ostrich feathers brightly dyed on their heads, and the men carrying their ox-hide shields and waving their knobkerries. Here was shown that those experts were right who said at earlier performances in Zululand and elsewhere that native dancers required time to warm

up. The Swazis of Westaffin had several hours to wait before the White Train arrived, and they spent the whole time dancing, watched by early arrivals who had come on the Pilot Train. Hour after hour they kept it up, stimulated by the steady rhythm of the tom-tom. Their fellow workers sat still and silent all through the morning to watch them; and the dancers themselves, far from showing any sign of fatigue, worked themselves up to ever livelier feats of athletic prowess as the hours went by.

The result was that the performance was at its best when the Royal Family saw it. They were, in fact, at luncheon when the train arrived, and were not ready to show themselves for an hour; but the natural good manners of the Swazis precluded any sign of impatience; the dance went on and the native spectators sat silent as before. When at length the royal party emerged from the train they were given a rapturous welcome, with cries of "*Bayete*," and moved for some time among the dancers with evident pleasure. Before leaving they were taken to see the Government's Research Station for the study of sub-tropical fruits, and the King, who in England has always taken a special interest in agricultural affairs, inquired closely into the important work which is being done at the station in furtherance of the great local industry. For Westaffin stands near the centre of a famous fruit-growing district, where not only tomatoes and mangoes are produced on a great scale, but also oranges, lemons and grapefruit, guavas and pawpaws and other succulent growths. To a visitor from rationed England this was indeed a land flowing with milk and honey.

March 29. And so at last the King of the Union of South Africa, with his Queen at his side and his daughters with them, came to his administrative capital of Pretoria. This was the culmination of their progress and their pilgrimage. In the Cape Colony they had trodden in the steps of Bartholomew Diaz and Vasco da Gama and Drake, of Van Riebeek and the 1820 settlers, and seen the melting pot of races in the tavern of the seas. Natal had shown them a people clinging tenaciously to their island origins even while playing their part in the building of a new nation far away from what they still called home. In the Orange Free State they had had a full introduction to that other equally proud culture which looks back to

a different European tradition and remains so jealous of its separate rights. But it was the people of the Transvaal who a century ago travelled farthest and endured most in order to vindicate their claim to live their own life untrammelled by the innovations of the newcomers to the land; and it was only in Pretoria that the Royal Family could be sure that they had penetrated at length into the innermost shrine of Voortrekker patriotism.

Pretoria became the seat of Government of the Transvaal Republic in 1860. Although it was founded by Marthinus Pretorius, who was the first president both of the Transvaal and of the Orange Free State, the name it commemorates is that of his father Andries, the victor in the battle of the Blood River. It was the headquarters for both republics in the early stages of the war of 1899; and it was its capture by Lord Roberts in the following year that brought the phase of large-scale field operations to an end, and reduced the conflict to a long-drawn-out guerilla. The city is full of monuments and buildings that recall the associations of the republican past, such as the old government buildings, the Palace of Justice, and President Kruger's house in Church Street West. The open space from which the main streets of the city branch out is dominated by the bronze statue of Kruger, with four Boer soldiers of the war period sitting on guard round the base. To one visitor, at least, in whose nursery the name of Kruger was a thing of mysterious terror, suggesting some diabolical monster with horns and tusks, it was a startling experience to see this venerable top-hatted and frock-coated figure, surveying the peaceful and spacious city with an air of stern benevolence. Time brings its revenges, and Kruger's city and even Kruger's own memory have been transformed into symbols of reconciliation. When the four Provinces which had fought one another in 1899 came together in 1910 to found a united nation, Pretoria was chosen as the principal scene of the great experiment; for it was here in the administrative capital, where government must be even-handed and unified, much more than in the Parliament at Cape Town, where the old rivals could fight their battles over again with words instead of guns, that the welding of the races must be attempted.

The supreme monument to the hope of a united nation is the noble range of buildings which Sir Herbert Baker, the great architect who accomplished so much of his finest work in South Africa, set upon the ridge called Meintjes Kop. These Union buildings house all the principal government departments in a spacious dignity which must in itself be an inspiration to all who work under their roofs. With their majestic courts and colonnades, they have a serene stateliness unequalled by any modern building in all Africa. In pictures they are familiar over the world, but no photograph has done justice to them, because it seems impossible to give an adequate idea of the splendid sweep of sloping lawns and terraces that reach up to them, past the replica of the war memorial of Delville Wood, from the open space at the foot of the hill where Steinberg's bronze figure of Louis Botha sits his horse and gazes afar into the veld. Round this statue of the beloved leader, who became the first Prime Minister of united South Africa, was formed up, when the Royal Family arrived there from the formal reception in Church Square, the most remarkable of all the gatherings they met during the tour. It consisted of over a thousand *Oudstryders,* which title is still proudly borne by the veterans who fought on the republican side in the South African War. Their bronzed and hardy faces, many of them wearing the full beards of the ancient fashion, suggested that even if they were not quite "that strength which in old days moved earth and heaven," the old commandos were still tough enough and patriotic enough to take the field again if the call should come. But if it came they were ready to stand shoulder to shoulder with those other South Africans by whom they had been defeated, but defeated with honour, half a century ago. Their great captain of those days, whose statue towered overhead, had shown them the way; their great living captain, who came now to bring their King among them, was still leading them in it.

As the ranks opened to receive King, Queen and Princesses and then closed about them while they threaded their way through the crowd, shaking gnarled hands and exchanging kindly greetings right and left, the feeling came over many who witnessed the moving scene that here at last the British Empire had overtaken the Great Trek. On what terms the two races are to share the land is still a question requiring all the resources of South

At Rhodes's grave

African statesmanship to answer. But here, in this revelation of instant affection and trust on both sides between the head of the Empire and the men who had once fought so gallantly to break away from it, was the evidence of the heartfelt desire that a united South African people should go forward under the ancient crown to the splendid destiny that a real unity of spirit must surely bring.

This reception by the *Oudstryders* took place in soft sunshine, which drew the utmost beauty from the green lawns sloping up to the Union Buildings. Unhappily a drizzling rain had been falling earlier in the day and marred the official reception in Church Square; and in the afternoon a heavy downpour almost wrecked the Governor-General's garden party. It did not, however, prevent a large gathering of loyal citizens of Pretoria from coming to see their King and Queen even at the cost of the probable destruction of their new top-hats and summer dresses. In the evening the Royal Family attended a State banquet in the City Hall, where the King delivered one of the most moving of his speeches, and the brilliant company deeply appreciated the words in which he showed his understanding and sympathy with the Voortrekker tradition, the Afrikaner culture, and the religious faith in which both were rooted.

March 30. As a further evidence of this sympathy, the whole Royal Family next day, which was Palm Sunday, attended the morning service of the Dutch Reformed congregation in the Groot Kerk of Pretoria.

March 31. On the Monday Pretoria entered into the informal competition which had been going on among the greater towns of the Union ever since the demonstration by the children of Port Elizabeth. No fewer than thirty thousand boys and girls were gathered round the Loftus Versfeld grounds to receive the royal procession, which they did with enthusiastic cheers and the singing of both national anthems, together with other English and Afrikaans songs. The entertainment they offered was another symbolic pageant, but conceived on completely different lines from that of Durban. It consisted of a procession of bare-footed children, some of them apparently not more than four years old, representing the months of the South African year—in a succession naturally strange to a northern eye, since it began with the gorgeous summer flowers of January and worked round to a Christmas tableau in which the Holy Family were again surrounded with the emblems of a midsummer Bethlehem. The dramatic climax of this scene, in which a great flight of doves was released behind the figure of the Christ Child and went wheeling across the front of the royal platform and up into the cloudy sky, greatly delighted the King and Queen. They went on to drive through a gathering of coloured and Bantu children nearly as numerous as the Europeans, although here the salute took the form rather of awed silence than of the wild cheering that had preceded.

The afternoon was devoted to the principal military parade of the tour, which was held at the Army's headquarters at Voortrekkerhoogte. This stately parade ground was formerly known as Roberts Heights; but on the occasion of the centenary celebrations of the Great Trek in 1938 General Hertzog's Government removed from the official map the name of the English general to whom Pretoria had surrendered. The old name, however, still survives in conversational usage.

Fourteen South African regiments had paraded contingents to receive new colours from the King's hand; and they showed by the proficiency with which they went through the historic ceremonial that a young country had no reason to fear comparison in its capacity for soldierly ritual with those in which this austere pomp had been developing through the centuries. Seven King's colours and seven regimental colours were laid on the piled drums of their respective regiments. They were blessed in simple form, some by Anglican and some by Dutch Reformed chaplains, some in English and some in Afrikaans. An officer marched along the line unfurling the flags, and they were finally delivered by the King himself into the hands of the kneeling ensigns. At the close of the rite the colours were marched past the King, and remained lined up across the parade ground while His Majesty presented war decorations to a large number of men and women of all ranks. After the storms of the week-end an afternoon of brilliant sunshine drew special glory from the crimson and gold of the colours, and made the most of that combination of strength with elegance through which military pageantry, supported by martial music, gains its peculiar power

Bechuanaland: the Guard of Honour

to uplift the heart. In a short and simple speech after the presentation of the colours the King showed his sense of the proud military achievement of his South African Forces, recent in origin, but rich in glorious deeds, which these emblems of regimental fame sustain, represent, and hand down to posterity.

Government House, Pretoria, was the headquarters of the Royal Family for the whole of Holy Week, although as will be seen they spent much of their days outside the city. They learned to know its peculiar atmosphere, which blends the pride and dignity of a capital, the sense of history that belongs to a community who are conscious of being in some sense pioneers, and the homely virtues of men and women who are, before all else, tillers of the soil, living in daily contact with the forces of Nature. It is a city of spacious streets that amble gently up and over the hills to a wide countryside where there is unlimited room to expand without danger of overcrowding. Great and splendid as are its most famous buildings, the beauty of the city as a whole is a beauty of landscape rather than of architecture; or at any rate its architects have conceived it their mission to reveal and embellish the natural beauties of the land. And it was in that spirit that the citizens of Pretoria adorned their city in honour of the King. The many-coloured lights in its centre, the floodlit Union Buildings on the outskirts, and the fireworks on the night of the royal arrival, all served to illuminate the romance of these lovely square miles of the high veld, where man still feels himself a sojourner even though for a time he wreathes it with the affections of home. So also when they had to entertain their Sovereign within doors, their instinct was to make their halls of state redolent of rural things. Many a building in the course of the tour had been transformed for the royal visit into the likeness of a garden; but for one at least of those who were privileged to accompany Their Majesties the banked flowers in the City Hall at Pretoria remain in this kind the most beautiful memory of all. South Africa laid little before the Royal Family to show that this young Dominion can yet challenge comparison with an older world in the domain of the fine arts. That is for the future. It made up for any deficiency in that regard by the great capacity of its people to perceive the riches of natural beauty with which their country is endowed, and to gather of their best for a royal offering. Nowhere was that sense of the beauty of nature more apparent than in Pretoria.

April 1. Thirty miles south of Pretoria there thrusts itself out of the high veld a barren range of hills known as the Ridge of White Waters or Witwatersrand. Here in the year 1884 a certain Mr. F. W. Struben picked up a crystalline pebble in which he detected signs of a richer mineral than quartz. Within a year adventurers from every country of the world were flocking in their thousands to the Witwatersrand, lured by that most avid of human passions, the insatiable hunger for gold.

In the sixty-two years since the army of speculators began to burrow underground along the Reef, the mining shacks that they hastily ran up as soon as they had pegged out their claims have given place to a city of solid concrete, containing a population of seven hundred and fifty thousand, which is easily the largest of any town in Africa south of the Equator. Yet this vast industrial conglomeration of Johannesburg still curiously retains the aspect and outlook of a mining camp. Though its greatest buildings flaunt the pride of the wealthiest city in South Africa, there is much also that is flimsy and ramshackle, and still seems to speak the mind of the early prospectors, whose life was always hung precariously between the poles of opulence and beggary. Even from the central streets, one can still look up to the gaunt ridges and dumps of the Rand. No one can ever forget for a moment the yellow metal on which the existence of the city depends, even if the daily conversation of Johannesburgers did not turn so persistently upon the rise and fall of gold-mining shares. Withal they make no apology for their preoccupation; they have worked long and laboriously to win the prosperity they enjoy, and they are very conscious that their city and its industry sustain the fabric of South African economy and contribute the lion's share of the public revenue. The world clamours for gold; Johannesburg can supply it, and in return holds the world to ransom for the enrichment of the Union as a whole.

With all its wealth and its teeming population, however, Johannesburg is not a provincial capital, and possesses no great official residence which it

Bechuanaland: native ornament bought at a casual halt

can use to lodge a King. Accordingly the Royal Family continued to sleep at Government House, Pretoria, and drove in to Johannesburg to meet its people except on the first night, when the White Train was brought to a siding near the city. If Johannesburg thought that it lost something by this arrangement of the programme, the Royal Family themselves certainly gained, for the drive across the thirty miles of veld, particularly on the return journeys at dusk, when the changing lights brought innumerable shades of lovely colour to deck the hill-tops and the shadows below, had not been surpassed for varied beauty in any of their journeys by road.

The effect of this manner of approach was that the Royal Family, in contrast to their usual routine, came first into contact with some of the native inhabitants of the outskirts of Johannesburg. The great demonstration which the city was preparing began, indeed, far back on the veld, at the native township of Alexandra, which had lately been the centre of Union-wide interest as the scene of an attempt to solve the housing problem with the high hand by a "Squatter" movement, evidently copied from that of the previous year in London.

For the moment, however, the fierce controversy was suspended, as squatters and permanent residents came out together to greet the royal party. A choir of children was lined up by the road singing "Nkosi Sikelel'i Afrika," and a small fife band, wearing kilts of Royal Stuart tartan, was playing Scottish airs with a gusto suggesting that though faces were black hearts might still be Highland. This was the beginning of a continuous parade of loyal enthusiasm that went on for mile after mile, as the procession moved through hamlets that joined themselves together and became suburbs, and eventually into the streets of the city. It might have been thought that the entire million population, not only of Johannesburg but of the whole Rand, had come out to join in the welcome.

Outside the City Hall and in the squares adjoining it crowds were packed in impenetrable masses; many thousands had been sitting on the pavements the long night through. Their cheering seemed to have a shriller note than that of Durban; but wild joy was the tone of it. Jubilation, however, was suspended for a few minutes, while the King stopped at the City Hall to unveil a new inscription on the Cenotaph, and the trumpeters of the Imperial Light Horse summoned the throng

Disembarking in Northern Rhodesia

to graver thoughts with the noble melancholy and unquenchable hope of the "Last Post." After tea with the town councillors within, the Royal Family appeared on the balcony of the City Hall to acknowledge the rapturous cheers of the crowd; and the King then came down to the top of the steps to review the parade of the war veterans of the Rand, both those still serving and the ex-service men and women. As befitted so great a centre of population, this was the largest such parade that the King saw in South Africa. Fifteen abreast they came swinging down the broad street, marching with an elasticity all the more remarkable because many of those in civilian dress appeared to be septuagenarians at least. There was a pleasant incident when the Alsatian mascot of the Royal Air Force saluted with loud barks the Shetland pony of the Imperial Light Horse, whose trumpeters were still at their post beside the Cenotaph. The marchers included all the races of the country, both European and native, and wore the medals or ribbons of all South Africa's wars.

In this crowded morning the King and Queen still found time to perform the ceremonial opening of the Rand Agricultural Show and inspect the winners of all the cattle classes, before attending the first of two civic luncheons in the City Hall; and in the afternoon they drove through many miles of native mine-workers in their compounds on their way to see the race for the King's Cup at Turffontein. The long day ended with a State banquet, and with a separate dinner party for the Princesses, who were to go on to a dance given in their honour for the younger people of Johannesburg. The King and Queen after dinner were taken up to the top of an eleven-story building to watch the fireworks; but the banquet had lasted longer than had been expected, and the fireworks were all over before they got there. So they went to the Princesses' ball instead, and stayed for an hour, eventually leaving their daughters to dance indefatigably on until the small hours of the morning. This had been probably the most exhausting day of the whole tour; a member of the Household described it as Becher's Brook the second time round. But the King, the Queen and the Princesses all came up smiling next morning for an almost equally arduous day.

April 2. They spent it driving through the long ribbons of satellite towns that stretch in both directions outwards from Johannesburg along the great gold-bearing Reef. The morning's journey was along the East Rand, and the afternoon's along the West. Making light of the dust, the royal party travelled all day long in open cars, and covered altogether about a hundred and twenty-two miles, breaking the journey at the City Hall for a second civic luncheon, at which the King made a short impromptu speech.

The landscape all along the Reef consists of bare sandy hills, some of them put there by nature, but others thrown up by the hand of man. These latter are the great towering cones of waste material from the gold mines, and exactly resemble the slag heaps so familiar in the mining districts of northern England and South Wales, except that they are nearly white instead of dark grey. The road runs straight and unfenced between them; and along it at every mine and location of the hundred miles were ranks of native workers, drawn from all over the Union and High Commission Territories, whose grinning black faces testified to the happiness brought to thousands of simple people by the visible presence of a Sovereign who had hitherto been as remote and mysterious as if he had lived in the moon. All day long the King and Queen went on acknowledging the salutes with a smiling grace that looked as fresh and unforced as if each village they passed was the particular one they had travelled ten thousand miles to see.

It was during the morning's tour of the East Rand that there occurred the only incident of the entire tour of the Union which for a moment seemed to be the expression of disloyal or unfriendly feeling. An excited Zulu came charging out of the ranks and bore straight down upon the royal car, which owing to the pressure of the crowds was moving at a slow walking pace. He looked as if he was bent upon attack, and the Queen with a smile on her lips, but determination in her eye, had to fend him off with the point of her sunshade. On inquiry, however, it turned out that this apparent rebel was yet another devoted patriot, whose only desire was to press a ten-shilling note into the hand of the object of his particular adoration, Princess Elizabeth.

The day's journey gave the Royal Family a vivid idea of the magnitude of the crowded industrial heart of a half empty land and of the vast significance of the golden foundations upon which the

Union of South Africa has built so large a part, as some think dangerously large, of its national economy. Some of their impressions of the pulsating energy that circulates from Johannesburg through the economic arteries of the nation came out in the King's speech at the civic luncheon, in which, after congratulating the citizens of Johannesburg upon the astonishing progress their community had made even within living memory, he added that he could not even now speak of the maturity, but rather of the vigorous youth, of Johannesburg.

April 5. The official programme had allotted the Royal Family a free day on Easter Eve, and one that they had abundantly earned. They decided, however, to give up their rest in order to pay a third visit to the city in which they had been so rapturously received. After a morning devoted to two great gatherings of school children, twenty-seven thousand in all, from whom they heard songs as typically English as "John Peel" and as South African as "*Sarie Marais,*" they went on to seek first-hand knowledge of that great source of mineral wealth with which the fortunes of

Bechuanaland: the Girl Guides

their South African people are so inextricably bound up. In a word, they went down the Crown Gold Mine. The King, the Queen, the Princesses and the Household were fitted out at the mine offices with long white coats and protective helmets, and thus clad were carried in two stages down one of the deepest shafts in the world. The cage descended at a rate of three thousand feet a minute to a depth of seven thousand seven hundred feet; but as Johannesburg stands five thousand seven hundred and thirty feet above sea level, they were not even then so far below the sea as are some of the comparatively shallow coal mines of Cumber-

land. At the foot of the second shaft was waiting an electric train of three or four diminutive coaches, in which there was just room for the party to sit, with the heads of the taller members bent to avoid the ceiling. The journey to the working face was about half a mile, and there the Royal Family watched with intent interest the work of the native labourers, who sat in strangely contorted attitudes, with their pneumatic drills, in the pockets of rock overhead. These pockets, where the miners bore and blast their way into the great Reef itself, which slopes down from the surface into the unknown depths of the earth, are curiously suggestive of the ovens of Malebolge, where Dante's imagination appointed the punishment of the simoniac Popes; but the native miner, hardier than Boniface VIII, can apparently acclimatize himself to anything, and those whom the King and Queen watched looked happy in their work. Farther on, the royal visitors were invited to look through glasses down a sloping haulage shaft, which was still under construction and followed the incline of the Reef itself. At its foot they could see the laborious diggers two hundred feet below driving painfully downward, with the intention of eventually following the Reef to the prodigious depth of nearly ten thousand feet.

After luncheon with the mine officials in a tent erected at the surface, the Royal Family went on to visit Baragwanath Military Hospital, which is maintained to give treatment in the sunny South African climate to patients from the United Kingdom Forces, mostly affected with tuberculosis. These sufferers, many of whom had been separated from their native country and their families for years, were inclined to welcome the visitors not only for their sovereign dignity but as emissaries

Lobatsi: Princess Elizabeth talking to native guides

bringing with them the atmosphere of home. The painstaking officials of the hospital had worked out with the precision dear to the army an elaborate programme, laying down the exact time to the minute to be spent over each stage of the royal progress through the wards. But the Queen is a poor subject for arithmetical computation. Their careful calculations went by the board as Her Majesty paused at every bedside and saw that each separate patient had his own share of the royal sympathy. So it was under a westering sun that the party emerged at last upon a quiet lawn, where the convalescents were assembled in a square to watch the King confer decorations on the commanding officer and the matron of the hospital, and on several patients who had won them in action. Night had fallen before the Royal Family returned to keep their Easter feast in Pretoria.

April 3. In order not to interrupt the description of Johannesburg's welcome to the Royal Family, it has been necessary to depart from strict chronological order and postpone mention of one expedition that they made from Pretoria. Accompanied by the Administrator and by the Minister in Attendance, Major van der Byl, they went by air on Maundy Thursday to the town of Pietersburg in the Northern Transvaal. In the course of the flight the leading Viking, which was carrying the

King and Princess Margaret, collided with a vulture and dented the fabric of its own nose. The planes passed over the northward limit of the pilgrimage of the Voortrekkers, who, supposing that they had reached Egypt and the head waters of the Nile, turned eastward from that point towards Laurenço Marques.

Pietersburg, which takes its Afrikaans name from General Piet Joubert, has an earlier history under the Bantu name of Polokoane, "the place of rest." It represents the sanctuary in which a native tribe, in desperate flight from the Zulus across the Drakensberg Mountains, at last found themselves safe from pursuit. It is still, in spite of its new industries of gold, asbestos, and corundum, the centre of a wide area in which tribal life thrives, and from which more than half of the native recruits to the South African Forces of the last war came. Here, at what was practically the extreme limit of their South African dominion, the Royal Family drove through four miles of cheering streets, attended European and native gatherings in the customary form, and were greeted with thunderous shouts of *"Pula,"* by which sonorous salute many of the Bantu peoples hail their King as the greatest benefactor parched Africa can know, the bringer of rain.

RHODESIA AND BECHUANALAND

*A*PRIL 7. When the Royal Family made their Easter Communion in the private chapel of the Bishop of Pretoria, their circuit of the four Provinces of the Union was to all intents and purposes completed. What was to follow in the last week of their visit would be in the nature of an epilogue. Meanwhile, they had eight or nine days to spare for a visit to the other great territory of Southern Africa which owes allegiance to the Imperial Crown. In the public gardens of Cape Town stands the statue of Cecil Rhodes, with his hand outstretched to the northward and on the pedestal the inscription "Your hinterland lies there." In several other cities of the Union his figure in bronze or stone looks out in the same direction. Rhodesia is to-day the outstanding memorial to his genius, and to his dream of a British Dominion extending from the Cape to the

valley of the Nile. It was he who in 1890 conceived the project of planting a colony beyond the Limpopo River, which should at the same time set a limit to the northward progress of the republicans of the Transvaal and open up a British corridor through which his projected Cape-to-Cairo railway might pass. In that year the column of pioneers, led by his close friend, Leander Starr Jameson, set out with the great hunter F. C. Selous as their guide to march from Kimberley through the vast wildernesses of Bechuanaland and made their outspan at last on the spot where Salisbury Cathedral now stands. The city of Salisbury, where they first set up the administration of the infant colony in a single mud hut, has survived the terrible Matabele War of 1893 and the Matabele-Mashona Rebellion of 1896, and is now the capital of a country that enjoys every

Princess Elizabeth meets leper girl guides who had travelled by bus to see her.

power of a self-governing Dominion, except, for the time being, that of conducting a completely independent foreign policy. Beyond the Zambesi, in a more primitive land, the Protectorate of Northern Rhodesia is still a little behind its sister colony in progress towards full self-government.

It is six hundred miles from Pretoria to Salisbury, and the Royal Family made the journey by air in the morning of Easter Monday. They were received at the airport by Sir John Kennedy, the Governor, and Lady Kennedy, and, after a procession to Government House through enthusiastic crowds in which Europeans and Africans were more closely interspersed than was usual in the Union, they reappeared before noon in order to perform the State opening of Parliament. It was the third such opening that the King had conducted since he spoke in November from his oldest throne in the House of Lords at Westminster. The ceremony might stand as a parable to illustrate the wonderful adaptability of the forms of parliamentary government, which with such slight modifications can control the affairs of an ancient and complex society in an island off the coast of Europe and of this community of primitive Bantu, with a few European planters, industrialists, and officials to lead them, in the heart of central Africa. Although the Parliament of Southern Rhodesia has but a single chamber, in which a bare thirty members represent a population of less than two million of all races—for all may qualify for the vote on the same terms—every punctilio of Westminster that can be adapted was scrupulously observed. Sir Alan Welsh, the Speaker, wore the same black and gold state robe as his elder brother at St. Stephen's; the Serjeant-at-Arms led in the procession of members in English court dress with a mace copied from that of the House of Commons; and when all were assembled came the familiar simple cortège, the King handing the Queen to her throne with the same forms of courtesy as in every Parliament, large or small, in which he has the opportunity to preside.

With the customary invitation to the members, "Pray be seated," he proceeded to read the "Gracious Speech," thus formally indicating that the measures designed by Sir Godfrey Huggins's administration for this remote community were to be regarded as the King's policy, just as fully as those which are propounded at the opening of a session in the United Kingdom itself. The whole ceremony was over in twenty minutes, and the procession drove back to Government House, the royal car preceded and surrounded by an escort of Mounted Police, armed with lances, the blue and gold pennons of which gave them a gaily martial air, even surpassing that of their colleagues in the Union.

April 7–9. The remainder of the three days that the Royal Family spent in Salisbury were devoted to mainly social functions, the purpose being as always to allow the largest possible number of people to spend a moment in their presence, or at any rate within their sight. At an investiture held in the charming grass-covered courtyard of Government House no fewer than two hundred and forty-nine Rhodesians were decorated. To the garden party, which took place in the public park, the entire population of the city, European and African, was invited. An indaba was held on the racecourse, and medallions were presented to fifty African chiefs from Mashonaland, Namaqualand and Nyasaland (which lies outside the boundary of Rhodesia). These potentates, who were uniformly dressed in gowns of scarlet and blue showing a remarkable resemblance to the robes of Oxford doctors of philosophy, had been chosen for the faithfulness with which they had assisted the policy of the King's Government in furthering the social advance of their tribes.

At a parade of ex-service men the King met and talked to about fifty survivors of the original pioneer column of 1890, and was presented with a little gold axe, a copy of the badge of the pioneers. Another charming present was the brooch of platinum and diamonds, representing a flame lily, which was brought to Princess Elizabeth at Government House, in honour of her approaching twenty-first birthday, by six children—two European, one coloured girl, one Indian boy and two Africans. They were the representatives of all the children of the colony, who had subscribed for the present a maximum of a shilling each for European, Asiatic, and Coloured, and a penny each for African. It was the first birthday present the Princess had received.

The same day the King was presented by the Prime Minister with a set of the first volumes in the series on Rhodesian history which has recently

Kimberley: the Big Hole

is the principal centre of Rhodesian gold mining. In the morning the train stopped at Wankee, in the Southern Rhodesian coal field, and the Royal Family came out to talk to the crowds on the platform.

April 11. They arrived at the Victoria Falls Hotel, which was to be their home for the next few days, just before noon on Friday, April 11, and after greeting Sir John and Lady Kennedy, who had come on ahead to receive them, went out at once to get their first view of the grandest natural spectacle in Africa.

It is less than a century since the great Victoria Falls were first seen by the eyes of a white man, the illustrious David Livingstone, whose statue now looks out upon them from the river bank. Still to-day, as in 1855, when he brushed aside native superstitions and made his way on foot to discover the truth about the "smoking water" of which the people spoke with such awe, the traveller's earliest view is from five or six miles away, where he sees a mighty column of vapour hurled a thousand feet into the air, and never dispersed by any wind because it is perpetually replenished from below. When he comes to the brink he discovers how this strange phenomenon is caused. Straight across the path of the swift-running waters of the Zambesi, which here are more than a mile broad, there opens a sheer chasm in the basalt rock, into which the whole mighty volume

been inaugurated through the endowment founded by Sir Ernest Oppenheimer.

The two Princesses were also invited to attend a parade of the Rhodesian Girl Guides and Brownies, but arrived at the appointed spot to find themselves gazing at an empty hillside. Suddenly, however, a signal was given and guides appeared from behind every rock and tree and came rushing down the hill to form up before them.

At a reception given by Sir John and Lady Kennedy on the first night of the stay some nine hundred of the leading members of the European community had the honour of meeting the King and Queen.

April 10. On the morning of April 10 the White Train left Salisbury for a journey of twenty-four hours to the River Zambesi, which forms the frontier between the two Rhodesias. Stops were made on that day at the agricultural towns of Hartley and Gatooma, and at Que Que, which

Bultfontein: provisions for the *Braaivleis*

of the river crashes, and then must at the same time compress itself to a width of a hundred yards and turn sharply to the left in order to force its way through thirty miles of narrow gorges before it can again find a wider bed through which to resume its journey to the sea. The scene where this tremendous transformation and diversion of power takes place has a majesty and magnificence which no words have ever availed to convey to those who have been denied the experience of its actual sight.

The scenery of the Falls is as varied as it is impressive. Near to the lip of the great cleft the river is divided by islands into two unequal streams, which take the great plunge in very different ways. On the Southern Rhodesian side is the Devil's Cataract. Its aspect is as if the whole hillside were sliding in a great avalanche downward, and that hillside made entirely of water, which boils and foams and surges until suddenly the steep slope becomes a sheer drop and the seething mass of liquid shoots out into space to fall thunderously into the cauldron below. The Main Fall to the eastward presents a complete contrast, for here the river sweeps down to the edge in one steady current nearly a mile wide, and without any intermediate incline drops straight into the gorge in the mightiest curtain of water that the world can show. Here is no sense of violence or tumult, only of the stately splendour of irresistible power. Though millions of tons of water are moving downwards, as they have been moving for centuries, with a terrifying velocity, yet the effect of the whole to the eye gives almost the impression of serenity and rest.

> "All is fixed
> In an eternal action, an eternal patience . . .
> That the pattern may subsist, that the wheel may
>   turn and still
> Be for ever still."

The Eastern Cataract, on the Northern Rhodesian side, has the appearance of a narrower segment cut off from the Main Fall, a ribbon or column of water tumbling downwards to add the last contribution to the infinity of foam in the "Boiling Pot" three hundred and fifty feet below.

April 11–12. The Royal Family visited the Falls on two separate days. They saw them under the sun and under the moon, from the level of the upper river, and from that of the gorge. They walked through the so-called "Rain Forest" opposite the Main Fall, where the spray forms a perpetual cloud, and where the King remarked that for the first time in his life he had been soaked even through his hat. They looked into the spray under the Eastern Cataract, where both solar and lunar rainbows arch themselves through the vapour; and they saw the little private rainbows that twinkle in and out of being for each observer as he moves. They saw, in fact, a dozen lovely or terrible aspects of the one great marvel; but like others they had little to say. In the face of this glory, this majesty of thunderous water, which has been tossing its foaming clouds of spume into the sky for thousands of years before English history began, and which in its panoply of power will reverberate down its gorges long after the British Empire has changed into forms unrecognizable—in the face of all this grandeur human royalty must needs bow in the same awe as reduces the humblest to reverent silence. Let Livingstone have the last word: "Scenes so lovely must have been gazed upon by angels in their flight."

Perhaps even the Victoria Falls would not have quite so overpowering an impact upon the mind if it were not for the contrast they present with the smooth swift stream of the river above. Only a few miles to the northward the great Zambesi, for all the speed of its current, can flow as broad and tranquil as the Thames at Runnymede. One might almost say that it was as gentle, but for the knowledge that unseen crocodiles lurk everywhere in its sinister depths. There is even a look of Runnymede about its islands, two of which had been named for the first time on the occasion of the royal visit, being called after Princesses Elizabeth and Margaret. This stately and peaceful reach, with its "pomp of waters unwithstood," was the scene of the entry of the Royal Family into Northern Rhodesia. From the point of view of watchers on the northern bank, where Sir John Waddington, the Governor of Northern Rhodesia, was waiting, the launch flying the royal banner came into view round the eastern end of the largest of the many islands, called Long Island; and simultaneously, from the mouth of the tributary Maramba, appeared the state barge of Imwiko, Paramount Chief of the Barotse, the largest group of tribes in Northern Rhodesia. This imposing

Ascent of Table Mountain

vessel, which had been brought three hundred miles downstream for the great occasion, was paddled by forty Indunas, in full ceremonial dress with lions' manes and red turbans. They are no ordinary ship's company: they are indeed the Paramount Chief's Ministers of State. Nor is their watermanship the least seriously regarded of their political duties; in former times a vacancy in the Cabinet

At the Birthday Review

father, Lewanika, the Paramount Chief who first placed the Barotse under the protection of the British Crown fifty years ago. Still more significant for the future was the presentation of a second address by an African clergyman at the head of the eleven notables forming the African Council; for this body is charged with the responsibility for selecting two Africans who next year will be the first

might result from clumsy paddling, for the offender might be thrown then and there to the crocodiles. "That puts ideas into my head," said the King, when the custom was explained to him.

Throned amidships under a great white canopy was the Paramount Chief himself, a man of sixty-five, who was partly educated in England, and succeeded to his constitutional monarchy on the abdication of his brother, Yeta III, in 1945. The gorgeous vessel fell into position as escort on the starboard side of the royal launch; and others only less magnificent joined the flotilla, one of them carrying the Murena Mokwai of Barotseland, who has the status of a Chieftainess, ranks next after the Paramount, and has her own court with similar state to his. A lady of Etonian connexions on the landing stage aptly compared the procession to a barbaric version of the Fourth of June.

After their picturesque approach to the Northern Colony the Royal Family were received on a platform in the principal street of the town of Livingstone, where dignitaries were presented in the usual form, went on to a garden party, and ended the day by presiding over an African indaba. At this ceremony the principal address of welcome was presented by the Paramount Chief himself, wearing a magnificent uniform like the frock-coat of an admiral, but of dark green instead of blue, with cocked hat and rich embroidery of gold lace. This resplendent costume was the same that had been worn at the coronation of Edward VII by his

of their race to take their seats in the Legislative Council of the Colony. The King having presented medallions to the principal chiefs and inspected the guard of honour, the indaba closed with the national anthem and repeated declamation of the Barotse royal salute, "Yo Sho, Yo Sho."

The visit to the Zambesi had been taken in a leisurely way and treated as a holiday for the Royal Family; and they found a good deal of the holiday spirit surrounding them the following week in Bulawayo, the chief commercial centre of Southern Rhodesia. Its wide and airy streets, which Jameson directed should be laid out so broad that a wagon with a full team of oxen could turn in them, had as gay an air as any that were traversed in the whole tour; and there were three miles of them to pass, with crowds cheering all the way, before the procession from the station reached Government House, where half a century ago stood the kraal of Lobengula, last and not least remarkable of the savage autocrats of central Africa.

April 14. The first day in Bulawayo will be remembered for the beauty of the flowers with which the citizens, triumphing over severe drought, had adorned their public park for the garden party; for the King's meeting with survivors of the pioneer column that overthrew Lobengula in the Matabele campaign of 1893 (among them Mr. Moffat, the former Prime Minister); and for a particularly delightful reception by the Governor and Lady Kennedy, which took place that night mainly on the lawns of Government House.

April 15. Driving out next day from Bulawayo into the heart of Matabeleland, the King held an indaba in the wildest and most rugged scenery of the tour. About fifty Indunas in the now familiar scarlet and azure gowns were present to receive him and many of them were given commemorative medallions. The echoes reverberating round the rocky kopjes gave back the King's voice with a strange suggestion of eerie solemnity, as he spoke words of sympathy for the Matabele people's sufferings in the drought and of gratitude for their loyal service during the war. Afterwards, having driven five miles farther still into the wilderness, the Royal Family left their cars to make on foot their pilgrimage to the bald hill-top which has been set apart as a burial ground "of those who have deserved well of their country." This lonely height, whose summit is strewn with enormous granite boulders of twenty feet or more in diameter, was called by Cecil Rhodes "View of the World"; and here in the midst of the circle

of rocks his body was by his own desire laid on March 26, 1902.

The royal party climbed slowly up the slope, the Queen's shoes failing her on the way, so that Princess Elizabeth had to bring her own to her mother's assistance, and herself complete the climb in her stocking feet. At the top they stood for some time in silent reverence for the memory of the three famous South African statesmen who lie in this place of honour—Cecil Rhodes, Sir Starr Jameson, his lifelong colleague, and Sir Charles Coghlan, the first Prime Minister of the Colony of Southern Rhodesia. They saluted also the square tower which commemorates the heroism of the thirty-three men of the Shangani Patrol, who under Major Allan Wilson in 1893 fought to the death against the entire power of Lobengula's Matabele regiments, and whose epitaph is "there was no survivor." It is perhaps the most austere burial ground in the world; if there is anything about these graves that can carry the suggestion of a hope extending beyond death, it is left to the sympathetic imagination of the beholder. But the stern strength which enabled these men of authority and valour to defy fate is typified for

Coming of age: at the Review

ever by the naked dignity of their last resting-place. It was with the sense of having seen into some of the secrets of the human power that has been built into the fabric of the British Empire that the Royal Family came back to Bulawayo.

April 16-17. The sands were now beginning to run out, and the return journey of 1,350 miles to Cape Town had to be completed in four days. Its first long stage lay across the edge of the Kalahari Desert, which forms a large part of the widely spread Protectorate of Bechuanaland. The people of this country are near akin to the Basuto; they came under the protection of Mosadinyana, or the Little Woman, by which name they still remember Queen Victoria, in 1885. To-day they are governed under the authority of the High Commissioner, like the Basuto and the Swazis. In their swift journey southward the Royal Family had only time to spend one morning with their Bechuana subjects, of whom twenty-five thousand had come in from all over the country to meet the White Train at the frontier post of Lobatsi. Here among the rolling hills covered with bush the Resident Commissioner, Mr. Sillery, in the unfortunate absence of Sir Evelyn Baring through illness, received the Royal Family on a platform adorned with a superb specimen of Bechuana craftsmanship. It took the form of a huge carpet of lion's hide, perhaps thirty feet by twenty, in which were inset the complete skins of a lion, a lioness, and two leopards. After the official speech by the Resident Commissioner, the leaders of the European, African, and Indian Muslim communities each presented a separate illuminated address. That for the Africans was read by Chief Batoen of the Bangwaketsi tribe, a glittering figure in a scarlet uniform of the Dragoon Guards, which had been bestowed on his grandfather by Queen Victoria in 1895. Tshekedi, Regent of the Bamangwato, who had added a pair of gold crocodiles to the uniform of the Royal Horse Guards Blue which had been acquired by his famous father, Khama, on the same visit to England, was no less resplendent, but played a smaller part in the proceedings.

After holding the last large investiture of the tour, the King reviewed a parade of Bechuana ex-service men, while Princess Elizabeth walked up and down through about an acre of African Girl Guides, very upright, dignified, and well-scrubbed figures. While these formalities were proceeding the vast general company were moving on the outskirts of the parade with the freedom of a garden party; and it was pleasant to see with what ease and familiarity all the races represented mingled with one another. These people had come from towns and villages scattered over a radius of six hundred miles; but they seemed to meet as intimates, and the air of general friendliness had not been surpassed in any place visited during the tour.

After a morning tea party in tents adjoining the indaba ground the White Train ran on into Union territory again, and came in the afternoon to Mafeking.

HOMEWARD BOUND

APRIL 17. The Royal Family were now once more in the Cape Province, and Mr. Carinus, their first friend among the Provincial Administrators, rejoined them, together with Mr. Senator Conroy, Minister of Lands, as Minister in Attendance. Mafeking is a small town, but its name is written large in history. It clings to its memories of the famous siege, and veterans of both armies that contended for its possession were standing together as friends on the steps of the town hall to give the Royal Family a rousing welcome. Inside, where the indispensable morning tea party took place, a striking decoration was the tattered Union Jack that flew over Baden-Powell's headquarters in 1899 and 1900. The building from whose cellars he directed the desperate but successful defence is still in use as Dixon's Hotel; and the royal procession drove past it after tea in the course of their peregrination of the principal streets of the town. Mafeking's welcome was genial and indeed affectionate; to be quite frank it was almost rowdy, and there was some evidence that the bars may have opened early in honour of the royal visit. There was good reason to remember the source from which the verb "to maffick" found its way into the English language. But the Royal Family took the rough humour of the town in good part, evidently perceiving that the inspiration of

With Field-Marshal Smuts and Mr. Hofmeyr on Table Mountain

it all was the unmistakable spirit of reconciliation that pervaded this focal scene of the feuds of long ago.

April 18. Last of all the major towns of South Africa to make the acquaintance of the Royal Family was Kimberley, another of the great fortresses that held fast in the South African War, but one whose military fame takes second place to that of the great industry which existed before the war and still thrives. The diamonds of Kimberley were drawing adventurers to South Africa long before gold was discovered on the Rand; and the foundation of the immense personal power of Cecil Rhodes was laid when he brought about the amalgamation of the two principal mines and so created the practical monopoly of the production of South African diamonds which is still enjoyed by De Beers. Sir Ernest Oppenheimer, the present chairman of this celebrated company, himself guided the royal party to see the great Kimberley mine, popularly known as "the Big Hole." He explained that both this vast funnel-like cavity, thirteen hundred feet deep, and the original De Beers mine which Rhodes amalgamated with it, were now exhausted, and work had been transferred to deposits that Rhodes described as "too poor to work, too rich to ignore." The thousands of uncut stones, representing a month's output, which were subsequently shown to the royal party at the office of De Beers, certainly suggested that the first half of this judgment was unduly pessimistic. The party spent some time looking down into the blue water which fills several hundred feet of the bottom of the pipe, while native boys threw stones into it, the sound of the splash coming back up the funnel in a strange echoing rumble about sixteen seconds after the throw. Before leaving in the afternoon for the last stage of the long overland journey, Princess Elizabeth was presented with a magnificent diamond weighing over six carats and enclosed in a casket made of the "blue ground" of the mine, while one of four carats in a similar case was given to Princess Margaret.

That night the royal party came back to the quiet vineyard on the Breede River where they had spent the first night of their journey two months before. The White and Pilot Trains earlier in the evening had drawn up together in a deserted place, and the King, Queen, and Princesses had taken leave of the passengers of both,

from the general commanding the police down to the native bedding boys, presenting to them all signed portraits or commemorative medallions. At the Breede River a good deal of informal hospitality was exchanged between the two trains, and the revelry went on far into the night.

April 20. In the morning, after a short stop at Beaufort West, the centre of an important sheep-farming district, the White Train steamed to its last stopping place at the Duncan Dock, under the shadow of H.M.S. *Vanguard* lying at the quay, whence it had set out on its journey of ten thousand miles. The Governor-General, the Prime Minister, and all the Cabinet, with their wives, were there to welcome the Royal Family home; and a true homecoming it was, for in the course of these last two months the Royal Family and the families of the South African Ministers had come to know one another as friends. The conversations on the quay were short, informal, but intimate; and within a few minutes the procession had formed and driven by the shortest way back to Government House, whence the Royal Family, since the day was Sunday, went immediately to the cathedral. The Cape Town crowds lined the streets once more to watch their progress, and cheered them all the way.

April 21. Monday, April 21, was the day when Princess Elizabeth came of age. It was entirely appropriate that so great an event in the life of the Royal Family should be celebrated, not at Westminster or Windsor, but in the midst of the loyal people of the youngest self-governing Dominion. Whether the dates of the royal journey had or had not been deliberately chosen for this purpose, the occasion emphasized in the face of the whole Empire the new constitutional fact that the Royal Family now belongs equally to all the sister nations of the Commonwealth, and that no one of them has a better claim than the others to enjoy any exceptional measure of the royal favour.

In the latter half of the tour Princess Elizabeth had stood out more clearly as an individual than in the earlier. Several times lately she had separated herself from the King and Queen and, generally accompanied by Princess Margaret, attended gatherings of Scouts and Guides and other ceremonies specially associated with youth. Her speech at East London had been broadcast to all parts of the Union, and helped the people to gain a clearer impression of her personality. Now, on her own personal festival, which had been declared a public holiday throughout the country, she stood forth more prominently than ever before. In the afternoon, accompanied by her own lady-in-waiting and one of the King's equerries, she took the salute at a march-past of the military garrison of Cape Town. It was properly treated as a ceremonial occasion of the first rank; the Prime Minister in his Field-Marshal's uniform met her at the saluting base; and not only the Cabinet but the entire Diplomatic Corps, imperial and foreign, except the Danish Minister, who was in mourning for his King, was there to do her honour. The Princess, standing up in her open car, drove slowly round all the ranks of regular soldiers, civil defence force, ex-service contingents, nursing services, women's auxiliary forces, and cadet corps, and then took her place on the platform beneath her own personal banner to take the salute at the march-past. Throughout the proceedings she presented the ideal aspect of a future queen, holding herself always with the dignity of a soldier, yet also with the simple grace of a young girl. The ringing cheers with which the parade took leave of her were more than a loyal salute to the future of a dynasty; they were a greeting to a charming personality who had delighted the eyes and won the hearts of soldiers and spectators alike.

In the afternoon the Princess was received with similar enthusiasm at a rally of youth organizations at Rosebank. Then in the evening, sitting alone in a quiet room at Government House, she broadcast her birthday message to her father's subjects. Although her words were addressed to all the five hundred millions of the Imperial Commonwealth, they contained a special message for the people of South Africa. When she said that, even though six thousand miles from the country where she was born, she still felt herself at home, she might have been summing up not only for herself but for all the Royal Family the meaning and achievement of the tour. The King, the Queen, and their children had been taken to the heart of the people, and would henceforth be regarded as true South Africans. As the young voice, vibrant with sincere emotion, went out over the mountains and the veld, to be heard from Cape Town to Pretoria, from Durban to Bloemfontein, and in innumerable lonely farm houses in the vast expanses of the empty land, men, women and children everywhere could call up before their eyes the portrait of the speaker as a friend and leader whom they had seen and could feel that they knew. In her closing words she called upon the whole Empire to witness what she called her solemn act of dedication.

"I should like," she said, "to make that dedication now. It is very simple. I declare before you all that my whole life, whether it be long or short, shall be devoted to your service and the service of our great Imperial Commonwealth to which we all belong. But I shall not have strength to carry out this resolution unless you join in it with me, as I now invite you to do; I know that your support will be unfailingly given. God help me to make good my vow; and God bless all of you who are willing to share in it." The words rang out like a tocsin and a challenge, and to many millions who listened there came the sense that here was the leader who could march at the head of a nation's effort to overcome the menace of hard and perilous times. The silent response in innumerable hearts to the Princess's summons to share in her life's mission was without doubt instant and genuine.

Cape Town ended the day in a mood of high jubilation. A mighty display of fireworks was let off by the sea-shore, and the Princess came down to see them. She passed on to the City Hall, where a great municipal ball was being given in her honour, and where she received a birthday present of jewels from the hand of the Mayor. She could only stay a little time, for her own more personal ball was already beginning at Government House. The invitations here had been for the most part confined to the young people of the city and the Cape Peninsula. But no one was surprised to find the Prime Minister among them, nor was his presence incongruous, for at the age of seventy-six General Smuts has not ceased to be one of the brilliant young men of the Empire. Two days later, when the Royal Family made the ascent of Table Mountain by the cableway, they would find that the Field-Marshal was already there, having climbed on foot to meet them; and although they persuaded him to come down with them, he confessed that it was the first time in his life that he had used artificial transport in either direction. Now at the ball, standing with the Royal Family in the gallery above the heads of the dancers, in the hall where the King's throne had stood when he received the two Houses of Parliament on the first day of the tour, the Prime Minister on behalf of all the people of the Union made a graceful speech of congratulation to the heroine of the day, and presented her with a magnificent necklace of twenty-one large diamonds. Afterwards the Princess threw herself into the midst of the dancing, saw her parents off to bed about midnight, and then danced on into the small hours.

April 22. Next morning General Smuts, who is inclined to be the Pooh Bah of the Union of South

now in the full robes of the doctorate, the Queen addressed to Congregation the only formal speech she made throughout the tour. It was one of the most eloquent that South Africa heard from any member of the Royal Family. Speaking with deep conviction of the supreme mission of a university to inform and inspire a nation's life at the highest levels of its aspiration, the Queen defined the four cardinal virtues of the academic faith. They were, she said, honesty, courage, justice, and resolve; but beyond all these, she reminded her audience with grave simplicity, religious faith was the indispensable foundation of the learned life.

While the Queen was thus being admitted to

Departure from Cape Town

Africa, appeared in yet another of his official capacities, as Chancellor of the University of Cape Town. The business before the House of Congregation was to confer upon Her Majesty the Queen the honorary degree of Doctor of Laws. In a felicitous speech of welcome the Chancellor, wearing long blue robes embroidered with gold, dwelt on the associations of the University with the Royal House, and their enrichment now that they were enrolling among their graduates one who had exercised such an inspiring and harmonizing influence throughout the Union. Then he thrice tapped the Queen on her already capped head with another inverted cap, and bade the Vice-Chancellor invest her with the hood of the degree. Arrayed

membership of the oldest university of the Union, the King had been creating a new imperial precedent by himself presiding over a meeting of the Executive Council, the body which in the Union corresponds to the Privy Council in England, and of which the Cabinet is technically a committee. At this meeting he gave his royal approval to various executive acts of the Government, and to regulations promulgated under authority delegated by Parliament.

April 23. The Wednesday, the last complete day of the royal visit, was kept deliberately informal, and devoted mainly to taking leave of various people who had been brought in contact with the Royal Family or who, like the drivers of the

Government fleet of cars, had served them during the tour. In the morning, as has been said, the Royal Family ascended Table Mountain and in brilliant sunshine enjoyed a superb view, extending more than a hundred miles, of the Cape Peninsula and the three oceans by which it is washed. In the afternoon they appeared at a farewell garden party given by the Administrator and Mrs. Carinus. A comparatively small company, nearly all of whom were personally known to the King and Queen, had been invited; and the afternoon of informality and peace, enjoyed on tree-girt lawns under the very cliffs of the great mountain, charmingly closed the domestic side of the royal tour.

April 24. By contrast with the domesticities of the Wednesday, the day of departure had been planned in terms of solemnity and state. But it takes more than top hats and guards of honour to maintain the ceremonial atmosphere, and at every turn it was found that formal pomp was modified and softened by evident human feeling. Where two months before the Royal Family had been greeted with a courteous and hopeful loyalty, in which simple curiosity was probably a major ingredient, the leave-taking brought to the surface on both sides every sign of affectionate regret that belongs to the parting of good friends. The State luncheon, for instance, which was the last meal the Royal Family shared with their South African subjects, corresponded in form to the State banquet of reception in February; but although the place was the same and the company but little changed, the whole tone and temper of the gathering were altogether warmer. Everybody present seemed to be on familiar terms with everybody else. All round the City Hall guests who had come out from England in the train of the Royal Family were taking leave of friends they had made in South Africa, and exchanging promises to meet again in one country or the other. Everywhere were being repeated the Afrikaans words *"Tot Siens,"* which correspond to the *Au Revoir* or *Auf Wieder-sehen* of Europe. The words might have served as a text for the farewell speeches exchanged between General Smuts and the King.

"Your visit," said the Prime Minister, "has stirred feelings among us, and will leave memories behind, for which it is difficult to find adequate expression. Never in the history of this, your South African Dominion, has there been such a wave of personal and national emotion as your visit has stirred among us. The immediate experience has been tremendous, and its after effects will endure and become part of the history of this land. They will continue as a beneficent influence moulding our life as a nation. All the various sections of your people, of all races and colours, have been thrilled by meeting with the Royal Family, and their lives have been enriched by this experience of human contact on the highest level. Your visit has been a blessing to us, at a time calling specially for a royal blessing."

The Prime Minister went on to give the King a cordial message of sympathy and admiration to be carried home to the hard-pressed people of England; and gratitude for this final summing-up of the fellow-feeling between the two sister nations, which had been expressed so often during the tour, occupied a prominent place in His Majesty's reply. But his words were also instinct with pride in the great South African people who had been so enthusiastic in hailing him as their head.

"I admire the courage and vigour, the earnest-ness and spirit with which your people grapple with the task before them. Your people pride themselves on the European stocks from which they are descended. They are imbued with the high principles and standards which they have inherited from their parent peoples. On those principles and standards there is no reason to doubt that they will succeed in building up a great country with a high and honoured place, not only in Africa, but also among the nations of the world. . . . May South Africa advance from strength to strength, in justice and righteousness, and in happiness to all its people."

The King ended with the words *"Tot Siens,"* which were received with tumultuous applause, for on his lips they could scarcely have any other meaning than to imply that some day he would visit his South African Dominion again.

After these formal though warm-hearted orations, immense pleasure was given to the company when

Arrival at Portsmouth

the Queen rose, and in a few simple and un-rehearsed sentences offered her personal thanks to the women and children of the Union for their hospitality, and her tribute to the rich tradition of South African family life. General Smuts then handed to the King, the Queen, and Princess Margaret presents from the Government and people of the Union; and finally all four members of the Royal Family went up to a box overlooking the tables and waved their good-byes while the guests sang "For they are jolly good fellows."

Down at the Duncan Dock, meanwhile, H.M.S. *Vanguard* was getting up steam and making the last preparations for the voyage home. The stands all round, which had been left in their place since February, were once again crowded with people who had come to watch the solemnities of the arrival unfold themselves in reversed order. To the outward eye it was all very much what it had been two months before. But high summer had given place to autumn, the "table cloth" was drooping over Table Mountain, and the mood of eager expectation had been replaced by a gentle melan-choly and a sense that a unique national experience was coming to an end. But there was joy also over a great and glorious addition to the historic memories of South Africa, and over a new friendship made between Sovereign and people, which all felt was destined to endure. So it was among smiling faces that the Royal Family said their last farewells to the eminent South Africans assembled on the platform and that the King reviewed his South African guard of honour for the last time. The Governor-General and the Prime Minister, who had been the first to greet the King, Queen, and Princesses on their arrival, were also the last to say good-bye. "God Save the King" and "Die Stem" were played, and the Royal Family passed up the gangway into the ship. A few minutes later they appeared on the high platform above the forward gun turret, from which their distant figures had first become visible to South Africans.

As they stood there waving to the cheering crowds the gangway was removed and the cables cast off. A foot of water showed itself between the side of the *Vanguard* and the quay. As she very slowly gathered way, choirs on shore took up the songs to whose rhythm so much of the royal tour had moved—"*Sarie Marais,*" the hymn "God be with you till we meet again," the Skye boat song, "Will ye no' come back again?" and "Land of Hope and Glory." All these melodies had gained rich associations of sentiment from the happy occasions on which they had been sung; all of them had become links between the Royal Family and their South African people, and would have power to move their hearts in reminiscence in the years to come. Last of all, when the *Vanguard* was already slipping out into the middle of the harbour basin, came the loving pathos of "Auld Lang Syne."

Soon the tugs had swung the *Vanguard* round, and she was heading for the harbour mouth and the open sea beyond Table Bay. But before the change of direction carried out of sight the figures still waving from above the guns, the crowds hitherto seated in the stands broke away in one great cheering multitude and came running down to the waterside to shout and cheer in their last farewell. So it was a sea of faces and a forest of hands, reaching out as if to make a last contact across the water, that made up the last sight that the King and Queen of South Africa would have of their southern people, as the frigates *Transvaal, Good Hope,* and *Natal* took up their escorting position and the little flotilla steamed away to the northward. For those who remained behind the radiant and romantic experience was ending, a vision fading. After two months of living in a luminous mist, to-morrow's sun would shed once more the light of common day. But something great would remain to remind South Africans of the experience through which they had passed. They would feel a new sense of participation in the glory of a historic Commonwealth, a deeper brotherhood with all their fellow subjects who shared the heritage, and a richer understanding of the living bonds of nationhood by which they themselves, in spite of all the super-ficial divisions of their party politics, were bound together into one people under the Crown.

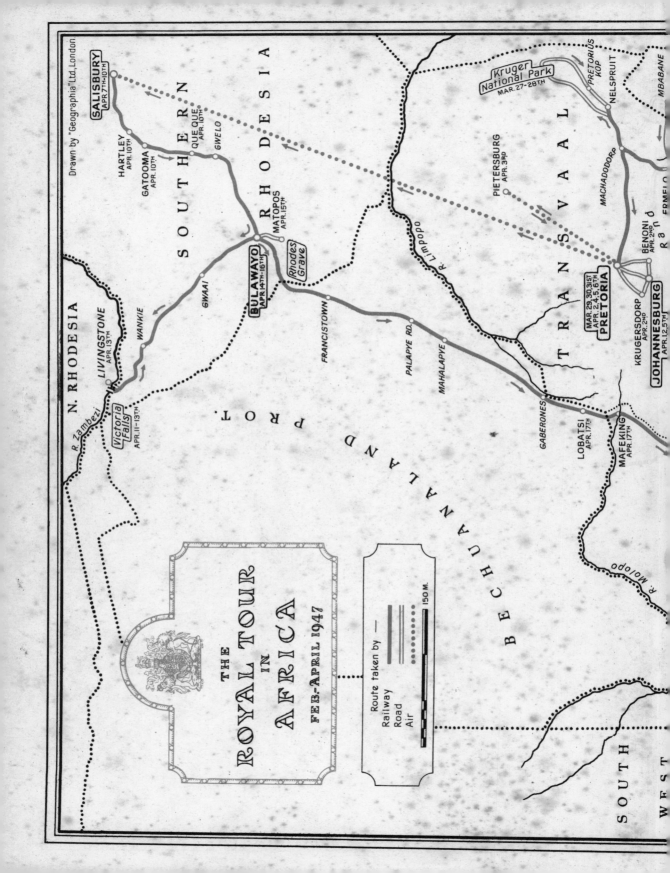

THE
ROYAL TOUR
IN
AFRICA
FEB.-APRIL 1947

Route taken by —
Railway
Road
Air
150 M.

Drawn by "Geographia" Ltd., London.

SALISBURY
APR 7TH-10TH

SOUTHERN RHODESIA

HARTLEY
APR. 10TH

GATOOMA
APR. 10TH

QUE QUE
APR. 10TH

GWELO

MATOPOS
APR. 15TH

BULAWAYO
APR. 14TH-16TH

Rhodes Grave

LIVINGSTONE
APR. 13TH

N. RHODESIA

WANKIE

GWAAI

Victoria Falls
APR. 11-13TH

R. Zambezi

FRANCISTOWN

PALAPYE RD.

MAHALAPYE

BECHUANALAND PROT.

GABERONES

LOBATSI
APR. 17TH

MAFEKING
APR. 17TH

R. Limpopo

R. Molopo

Kruger National Park
MAR. 27-28TH

PRETORIUS KOP

NELSPRUIT

MBABANE

MACHADODORP

PIETERSBURG
APR. 3RD

TRANSVAAL

PRETORIA
MAR. 29, 30, 31ST
APR. 2, 4, 5, 6TH

KRUGERSDORP
APR. 2ND

BENONI
APR. 2ND

ERMELO

JOHANNESBURG
APR. 12, 5TH

SOUTH WEST